Hester Pendleton

Husband And Wife

The Science of Human Development Through Inherited Tendencies

Hester Pendleton

Husband And Wife

The Science of Human Development Through Inherited Tendencies

ISBN/EAN: 9783744759038

Printed in Europe, USA, Canada, Australia, Japan

Cover: Foto ©ninafisch / pixelio.de

More available books at **www.hansebooks.com**

HUSBAND AND WIFE;

OR,

THE SCIENCE OF HUMAN DEVELOPMENT

THROUGH INHERITED TENDENCIES.

BY THE

AUTHOR OF "THE PARENT'S GUIDE," ETC.

"Science is the knowledge of many, systematically arranged and digested so as to be attainable by one."—HERSCHEL.

New-York:
CARLETON, PUBLISHER, 413 BROADWAY.
M DCCC LXIII.

To

The Mothers and Daughters of the Human Family,

TO WHOM IS INTRUSTED

THE CONTINUANCE OF THE RACE,

AND WHO

DESIRE THAT IT SHOULD BE DONE MOST WORTHILY,

This Book is Dedicated.

CONTENTS.

INTRODUCTION.

Woman, Nature's most trusted Agent in her highest Designs for the Race; Statistics of the last Census; Reports regarding Idiots, Mutes, the Blind and the Insane; these, and Infirmity of every kind are the Effects of Causes which Society can lay hold of and remove—Illustrated; An Appeal to the Women of the Nineteenth Century...... 13

CHAPTER I.

Intellectual and Moral Qualities Transmissible; Illustrated and Proved; Progress of Opinion on this Subject; Object of the Present Work; Importance of a Knowledge of the Laws of Inheritance; New Incentives to Self-Culture; Its Reward, the Development of a Higher Type of Humanity...... 17

CHAPTER II.

Influence of the Father on the Child through the Imagination of the Mother; Her Power over the young Immortal almost limitless; When, and how circumscribed; Value of high Health; Man no Exception to Nature's great Law of Development; What Influences the original Organism; Theory of Twins; When it will be verified; How to secure Noble and Worthy Offspring...... 21

CHAPTER III.

Consanguineous Marriages deprecated; Evil Effects not always present; Similarities of Temperament, of Organism, of Tendencies, frequent causes of Inherited Weaknesses; Case in point; Protean forms of Disease; Antidote; Mysterious Dispensations...... 25

CHAPTER IV.

Subject continued; Family Idiosyncracies, Mental and Physical; Defects, how intensified; Dr. How's Opinion; Some Statistics; What the Professor says; The Innocent punished through the faults of the Guilty.......... 29

CHAPTER V.

Geoffroy St. Hilaire; Monstrosity, Malformation, Idiocy and Imbecility not the result of a blind chance, but the product of a disturbed action of beneficent Laws of Nature; Verified by Experiments; A Knowledge of the subject the basis of Human Progress; An Appeal to Mothers.......... 35

CHAPTER VI.

A Chapter of remarkable Facts, corroborative of the Observations and Arguments of Saint Hilaire; Logical Inferences of a Contraband.......... 42

CHAPTER VII.

Mysterious Power of the Mother's Imagination in producing Malformations; When the Millennium may be expected.......... 53

CHAPTER VIII.

Fatal Effects of Exhausted Physical Strength on Offspring; Instances of Scrofula, Consumption, and Idiocy, induced by it; Precocious Children.......... 58

CHAPTER IX.

Reasons why we must expect fearful bills of Infant Mortality, and frightful evidences of Early Decline.......... 64

CHAPTER X.

"Men are what their Mothers made them;" Weakmindedness Hereditary; Causes of Insanity among the Ignorant, the Vicious, and the Intemperate; Among the Educated, the Respectable, and the Wealthy; Victims of Exhausted Mentality; Why the Sons of Great Men seldom become distinguished; Intellectual Vampires; Why they seek Social Intercourse.......... 68

CHAPTER XI.

The Progress of the Age shown by the Present Position of Women in Christian Countries; The Training of Boy and Girl contrasted; Its Results; As the Mothers are, so will the Children be; The Cynic's Question answered; The Advancing Tide of Human Progress; Woman's Participation 75

CHAPTER XII.

M. Michelet; The French Ideal Marriage a Poetical Fancy, repudiated by Reason and Experience; Woman not created an Invalid; The Laws of Nature Justified; The Child-wife a Fallacy; No True Marriage except between Equals; Opportunities for Higher Culture demanded for Woman; The American Ideal Marriage a Substantial Reality; The Wife's Mission 81

CHAPTER XIII.

M. Michelet's Audacity; Important Information for those who need it; A Gem from Carlyle; Questions put by the Inexorable; An Eastern Fable 86

CHAPTER XIV.

"New Theory of Population;" The Progressive, Unending. Development of the Race guaranteed by a Knowledge and Practice of the Moral and Physical Laws; Individual Responsibility in the Parental Relation; Children are Blessings only to the Worthy; Modifying Conditions which should Limit the Number of Offspring; Why Society is everywhere Cursed by the Weak, the Vicious, and the Improvident; Self-Control, Man's True Sovereignty; The Progressive Thoughts of the Age on that subject destined to pervade and elevate Society; Some of the Dark Streams flowing from the Great Turbid Fountain of Inheritance; Their Remedy safe and practical; Suggestions worthy of the Attention of those engaged in the Education of Youth 92

CHAPTER XV.

National Characteristics of Americans: Mind superior to Matter; A New Application of Domestic Economy suggested; The Bachelor's Reasons for not marrying; A Moral Necessity; Questions to be answered; Evil Effects of Attentions from Single Gentlemen to Young Wives; Suggestion on the subject, by Margaret Fuller. ...., ... 95

CHAPTER XVI.

Human Parasites; Nature's Retribution; The Converse of the Picture; Consolation.... 107

CHAPTER XVII.

The Causes of various Social Evils; The Probable Proportion of Children born who are cordially Welcomed by both Parents; The Evils of too Early and too Frequent Maternity; The Causes which produce the different characteristics of the Welcome and the Unwelcome Child; The Welcome Child; a Case proving the practicability of conferring desirable Qualities on Offspring; Further Illustrated by Facts from Scripture, from Modern History, A Plea for Wives, showing how Children may become more Beautiful, more Healthy and Harmonious in Body and in Mind; Man's Injustice or Selfishness towards Woman recoils upon himself, through a Degraded Offspring; Retribution, or the Domestic Nemesis.... 110

CHAPTER XVIII.

Highly Nervous Susceptibility one of the Distinguishing Attributes of Woman; Its Effect in the Maternal Relation; Illustrative Cases.... 116

CHAPTER XIX.

Facts more satisfactory than Arguments; Case of Mental and Physical Superiority of one Child over the others of the same Family; Its Causes.... 121

CHAPTER XX.

Moral, Intellectual and Physical Qualities can be predicated; How; Whom the Gods Love Die Young; Why; A Remarkable Musical Genius not Inherited.... 126

CHAPTER XXI.

A remarkable Case verifying the preceding Opinions; Reflections suggested by a Visit to the House of Refuge; Dishonest Propensities, when innate, How Transmitted; Seeming Anomalies; "Be sure your sin will find you out;" Illustrated by Interesting Facts.... 130

CHAPTER XXII.

Examples of Hereditary Intellectual Qualities descending directly from the Father; Blaise Pascal, the Bonheur Family, the Beechers, Theodore Parker, John Quincy Adams; the Powers of the last two Intensified by Able Mothers; A Scrap of Biography, a Study for Husbands, Wives and Sons. 137

CHAPTER XXIII.

Dr. Laycock on the Evolutions of the Human Brain and Mind; Inferences; What has given America her proud Position among Nations; How to Insure a Nation's Prosperity and Stability; The Effects of great Emotional Influences on a Nation; The great Generations appear as the fruit of such Influences; Exemplified; A Prophetic Glance into Futurity 144

CHAPTER XXIV.

Some Thoughts suggested by Darwin's "Origin of Species"; Man, by studying Nature's Methods in the Irrational World, may produce similar Effects in the Rational; Selection one of those Methods; This Principle may be applied for the Benefit of Humanity, and for the Progressive Development of the Race... 150

CHAPTER XXV.

"Natural Selection" has been gradually giving us gentler and more refined Races of Men; "Selection" the Magician's Wand by which he may summon into Life whatever Form or Mold he Pleases; The Whole Secret of Transmission; Why the Animals in Dark Caves are Blind; The Penalty for not heeding Nature's Laws. 156

CHAPTER XXVI.

Quotations from Prosper Lucas on Natural Inheritance; Transmitted Tendency to Drunkenness, to Insanity and to Suicide; Children Engendered in Drunkenness often Idiotic; This Subject understood by the Ancients 165

CHAPTER XXVII.

Certain Mental Qualities transmitted in Families; Instances of the Inheritance of Oratory, of Political Genius, of Poetry, &c.; Moral Resemblance of the Daughter to the Father, of the Son to the Mother; Cases 172

CHAPTER XXVIII.

Advantages of Health; Inefficiency of Sickly Scholars; From what Class the real Nobles, the veritable Leaders of Mankind, have to be recruited; Gradual Progress of Public Opinion and Popular Taste on this Subject; Benefits of Out-door Training for Girls; Examples 178

CHAPTER XXIX.

A brief Chapter upon the Every-day Unconscious Influences which are the great and permanent Molders of Character in every Age; An acknowledged Truism; How to truly Improve the Race; Magnetic Power of Emotional Attraction; Isolation Dwarfing in its Tendencies; Association the continued opening up of wider Experiences; Exemplified; Why Children so often disappoint the Hopes of Parents; To Promote a more Perfect Human Development 185

The Mother's Prayer 193

A copious Appendix, containing further Proofs of the Laws of Inheritance, together with much Knowledge needful to Women, Some of it quoted from the Writings of the most progressive Minds of the Age; Some of the Evils which desecrate Humanity, and impede a harmonious Development of Offspring. 197

INTRODUCTION.

The writer assumes in this volume that there are laws of hereditary transmission in the mental and moral, as well as the physical constitution. Precisely what all these laws are, she does not assume to state. Careful observation, and an earnest sense of their importance, must be employed for their full discovery. In the mean time, acquaintance with such as are known will be helpful to all, and will facilitate the discovery of those yet hidden from us. Women, who bear so important a part in parentage, should be the most clear-sighted students of Nature in these things. They know so much more from experience in maternity, than men can know in paternity,—the nearest of possible relations before birth is so exclusively theirs,—they are so exceedingly emotional, and appreciative of external influences bearing on themselves, and through themselves on the unborn, that much—most, in this department must naturally fall to them.

We have not only endeavored to give the facts for the law of maternal power, but according to the best authorities and the widest observation, have stated the law for the facts; so far, at least, as the mother's power during the period of gestation is concerned. The important points developed are, First, That the mother's intellectual activity, under certain circumstances, descends: Second, That her affectional state, if not overruled by some more powerful impressions, has a degree of influence almost determining in character: Third, That her susceptibility *as woman*, makes the choice of influences that shall co-operate with her maternal forces a momentous power in its results on her child.

We have also shown some of the physiological conditions that are the most influential to offspring. While scientific men dispute what these are, it behooves women, who love truth for its practical value in increasing human happiness, to take such as are known for their daily law of life. Society is directly concerned that they should do so, since its interests rest so largely in them; their children, also, have a sacred claim on them for protection against the wrongs which ignorance or apathy may inflict. If the mother forsakes them before she gives them birth, what power can restore their lost faculties or deficient energy?

In the year 1860, the governors of the States of Ohio and Kentucky, in their annual messages to the Legislators recommended and urged the enactment of a penal statute against the marriages of blood relations, on the ground that those States were already heavily burdened with the deaf and dumb, blind, imbecile, and idiotic offspring of such marriages. What a fearful betrayal of the weak and the helpless, who, innocent of all complicity in their own ruin, can get no redress, and have no appeal from the ignorance, the selfishness, or the mercenary spirit which has thus sacrificed them.

It is to woman that humanity must look for abatement of such frightful evils; for it is she who loves perfection,—who awakened in her consciousness, strives with the artist's yearning for it—with religious enthusiasm that it may appear. Nature's most trusted agent, in her highest designs for the race every individual of her sex is under a solemn obligation to every less enlightened one to bring her to a knowledge of the power with which she is clothed —of the legitimate results of its use, and the possible consequences of its neglect. Yet this, which ought to be a part of the instruction of every woman, is the last word she ever hears from those professing to educate and fit her for the duties, the responsibilities, and the privileges of life. Much that pertains to the same phenomena among the lower animals may very properly constitute a part of her studies in natural history, if she have a taste for it, but with the laws which govern the most momentous of all social effects—the moral and mental constitution of individuals composing society—with the gravest of possible results to herself—the embodiment of power or weakness, capacity or incapacity, worth or worthlessness in her own offspring, she is forbidden all acquaintance. Yet when she assumes the duties and the responsibilities of maternity, such knowledge would be more valuable to her and to those dearest to her, than all of the treasures of the gold-bearing lands of the nineteenth century, if poured at her feet.

Intelligent persons are learning in these days, that idiocy, and some of the physical infirmities, which fill our hospitals and asylums with armies of unfortunates, blighted in brain or in body, have causes which can be removed. Society does not now, as uniformly was its wont, lay all such calamities at God's door, and thus wash its hands of all responsibility touching them. But if idiocy, then imbecility also, and if imbecility then those degrees of inferiority which, less than either, are still sufficient to make their subject a burthen, rather than a help to the community to which he belongs.

The dependence of every fact upon some law, is predicable to the philosophic mind. Yet it is necessary to exhibit a basis of relation between the existing cause, and the manifest fact with which we are called to deal. This work treats of idiocy and inferiority of every kind as effects of causes which individuals and society can lay hold upon and remove. That they are such will be apparent to all who take the trouble to examine the testimony set forth in these pages.

Uniformity of appearance, development, and disappearance in any phenomena, are evidences of a law behind it, which laying near to common observation, is little likely to be denied. The Census returns of every country in Christendom, since statistics became a science, show a very uniform per-centage of idiocy and imbecility. It keeps pace with the increase and the decrease of population, and exhibits marked variations from these only when known and striking causes which might be expected to contribute to such results, have appeared. Thus according to Baron Percie, of ninety-two children born in the department of Landau in the month immediately succeeding the Reign of Terror, sixteen died at birth; thirty-three lived from eight to ten months; eight became idiotic, and died under five years of age; and two were born with fractured bones. Thus more than fifty per cent of these unfortunates were actually killed by the fright and agitation of the mothers. We know not how many among those who survived, were the subjects of less degrees of inferiority which they had to endure throughout their lives in consequence of the strong and terrible impressions upon the maternal susceptibilities. Here is seen on a large scale, the operation of causes which acting singly, lead to like results in the case of families and individuals.

The last Census reports of the United States exhibit respectively in round numbers, twenty-four thousand insane, eighteen thousand idiotic, fourteen thousand deaf and dumb, and eleven thousand blind among us—a fearful army for a nation of less than thirty millions, claiming to be, all things considered, the most enlightened people on the earth. When we reflect that in all probability many thousand imbeciles, barely separated by a scarcely appreciable development from idiots, escaped numeration, we may well begin to inquire for the remedies of this fearful state of things; and call to their posts those whom Nature has empowered to prevent such terrible evils. These are the mothers, the women of our nation: what they in their creative capacity, have left undone for their offspring, the idiot-trainer, the criminal Judge, or prison discipline, must do in their stead. for these victims of their ignorance or faithlessness.

It is time we should awake, women of the nineteenth century, to our duties and to our privileges as well. Never were such opportunities offered our sex before—never grew such noble fruit of earnest effort within our reach, as now hangs upon the branches of the tree of knowledge for us, to be gathered in fair womanly conscientious dealing towards those whom we love best on the earth—whose helplessness has no redress if we fail them—our unborn children. God so commend them, and through them, humanity, to our hearts and minds, that we cannot fail in our duty to either. God make our nation as great in its woman-hood, as it is in its political, civil and religious stature, since by the power of the first only, can the last be preserved, strengthened, and improved, from generation to generation.

HUSBAND AND WIFE;

OR,

THE SCIENCE OF HUMAN DEVELOPMENT.

CHAPTER FIRST.

More than twenty years have elapsed since this writer issued the first edition of a volume entitled "Mental and Moral Qualities transmissible from Parent to Offspring,"—a work that has been widely circulated, and which, as far as the author is aware, was the first extensive treatise on that subject. This book is now known under the title of "The Parent's Guide" —it dwells not only on the certainty, but it also suggests the means, of transmitting talent and virtue from parent to child.

It is there shown, that while education and habits subsequent to birth, are all important, yet, that transmitted hereditary qualities, give the original bias, which is never afterwards entirely overcome. And also, that the biographer must go further back than education, in order to elicit the true cause which produced pre-eminence in the subject of his memoir; for the Creator has given to man, his peculiar reasoning faculties, for the purpose, that *here as elsewhere,* he might acquire the direction of events, *by discovering the laws regulating their successions.*

The following paragraph is from this work:

"It cannot be denied that if the same amount of knowledge and care which has been taken to improve the domestic animals, had been bestowed upon the human species, during the last century, there would not have been so great a number of moral patients for the prisons, or for the lunatic asylums, as there are at present. That the human species are as susceptible of improvement as domestic animals, who can deny? Then is it not strange that man, possessing so much information on this subject, and acknowledging the laws which govern such matters, should lose sight of those laws in perpetuating his own species? Yet how extremely shortsighted is that individual who, in forming a matrimonial connection, overlooks the important consideration of the quality of the physical and mental constitution which his children will be likely to inherit? And also, that a great portion of the happiness or misery of his future life will depend upon the conduct of those children: and again, that their manifestations, whether for good or evil, will be the effect of the mental and physical organization which they inherit. The time is fast approaching when men will have to pay more attention to this subject; for a knowledge of Phrenology, the science which tests such matters, is rapidly spreading; consequently the parent cannot hope much longer to receive the sympathy of society for the perverse conduct of his child,—on the contrary, the child will be commiserated for having inherited active animal propensities, accompanied by deficient moral and reflective organs."

This prediction has already been verified; much attention has been directed to the question of transmitted tendencies, by some of the most profound observers and philosophical reasoners of the age. And the hitherto apathetic, are beginning to discard time-worn prejudices, and to look into the subject with interest and intelligence.

The present work is intended to supply the deficiencies of the previous one,—to collect, condense and put into popular form, some of the great truths contained in the recently published works intended exclusively for the medical profession, or for the natural philosopher. Its aim is also to take a much broader and more comprehensive view of the whole subject; to further develope other important laws on the transmission of desirable qualities,—to show how various occupations, circumstances and relations of life, help to modify the character of the parents, and that the offspring are thus inevitably affected by the whole past lives of their progenitors.

A deep conviction of the importance of these truths will make all of life full of the highest and most touching responsibilities—will give a new and direct impetus to the cultivation of good habits, and to a recognition of the necessity of preserving a sound constitution. All young persons must feel the stimulus of a great and unselfish motive, to the cultivation of their highest powers, and to the subjugation of their lowest propensities; they must be taught to look forward hopefully to lives which may be kindled into being—

sparks of immortal flame scintillated from their own pure natures.

It is thus, through our affectional and social as well as our devotional instincts, that the Almighty presents the highest possible motives for well-doing. The holy fire of self-sacrifice which is kept burning more or less brightly on the altar of every heart, is the noblest incense that we can offer to the Creator. We have only to appeal to this to show how it can practically secure the good it seeks, and many a generous sentiment will embody itself into form—and thus a new and beautiful human organization will spring into existence; and children born pure and good themselves, will become the worthy parents of a still higher type of humanity.

CHAPTER SECOND.

If the father of a child be one upon whom the mother's mind can dwell with enthusiasm, not only with ardent affection, but with proud admiration of his noble nature, then the offspring will be so many copies of the father—spiritualized and enlarged by the glorified imagination of the mother.

More than half of the children born into the world resemble the father more than they do the mother. As a holy and ennobling influence, or, as an unhallowed and disturbing one, he must be often present in her thoughts; she bears the impression of him in her soul during the whole ante-natal life of her child; therefore, his influence for good, or for evil, must be very great.

When attention is first directed to the improvement of the human race, it is natural that we should dwell largely upon the proper conditions of the mother. She seems more nearly related to the child, and her influence is more directly obvious. There are those who believe that the mother's power over the character of her offspring is almost omnipotent; hence they pay little attention to the father, and even assume that though he should be an invalid, an imbecile or a debauchee, yet the mother can make hers a model child, physically, mentally and morally. We would not underrate her power in any of these respects; it is almost limitless. What all the forces of Nature combined in the earth, the rain and the sunshine, can do for the young plant, that also can the perfectly healthy mother do towards nourishing her unborn child. This, however, is only the material portion of her work,— her higher human nature will also leave its divine impress upon the young immortal.

The value, then, of physical health,—of the most cheerful, inspiriting conditions of an active, self-reliant, mental life, on the part of the mother, can never be exaggerated. Her resolute will can do very much towards modifying and controlling all unfortunate circumstances; but she cannot work miracles, she cannot subvert the action of the organic laws. An oak tree will never grow from a beech nut, nor a rose spring from the bulb of a lily. So the Ethiopian is never father to a Caucasian; nor can a weak-minded man ever hope to become the parent of a strong-minded offspring. Favorable conditions may, indeed, work marvellously towards the development of a feeble germ,—we may nourish the weakest plant into something like vigor and hardiness, but one strong and rare seedling is worth many hundreds of any common variety. These analogies are full of meaning, for man is no exception to Nature's great law of development.

In the improvement of animals, we are already aware of the great importance attached to the pure blood of the male. Both parents unite in creating the embryo; it is the reproduction of neither; but if all conditions are favorable, it should be an improvement upon both. Nature is so intent on this result that in spite of the crimes, follies, and stupidities of the race, she has yet managed to bring up the tone of the general mind many degrees. Perhaps no child begins life on so low a plan, mentally, as did some of his dull phlegmatic ancestors. Compare the generation of to-day with even that of a hundred years since,—the present has greatly the advantage. We talk of inheriting the cultivation of a long line of ancestors; true, we inherit the results of their culture through the medium of the law of development.

The habits of the mother, and the accumulation of all other influences through her during the whole period of gestation, are of immense importance. Yet the previous habits of both parents are still more important, it is these that influence the original constitution of the future man,—one in nurturing the seedling, the other in determining the inherent character and organism. The functions being thus different, there can be no adequate comparison between them.

Education and nurture, both before and after birth, can do much for every child, but these can never makes a Shakespere, a Bacon, a Mozart, an Elizabeth Fry, or a George Sand. All great genius, strength, and originality of character must be inborn,—they cannot be superinduced by any subsequent culture.

We generally find a great similarity in all children of the same birth. A twin is a synonyme for marked resemblance. The same influences have operated upon these closely-united little lives—therefore the likeness in result. Occasionally, however, we find one blue-eyed, fair-haired, and gentle in character; whilst the other is dark-eyed, raven-haired, restless and vivacious. However we may theorize about causes, the differences, both mentally and physically, are organic. Were they conceived at different times, when the parents were in different moods—or did one take on the prevailing type of the father, and the other that of the mother?

When as much thought shall have been bestowed upon the organic improvement of the human species, as the horticulturist has given to his art, we may then learn something of the laws for the transmission of mental activity—of genius—of sameness or diversity of talent, and of all the transcendent powers of humanity.*

One general principle, however, may be laid down as infallible. He who has lived most in accordance with his whole complex nature—developing all his powers in the highest harmony, is best fitted to bequeath a like harmonious organism to his offspring.— But as there are two parents who bring this new life into existence, these two must assimilate and blend into the one, if they would make it a pre-eminently more exalted being than themselves. The brutes, with their fierce instincts, care for nothing higher— but these united intelligences must subjugate and transcend all mere animal propensities, if they would become the parents of a noble and worthy offspring!

* See Appendix A.

CHAPTER THIRD.

Much has been said and written upon the effects of consanguinity in marriage. It is generally thought that blood relationship is a great cause of imbecility and disease; statistics showing the frightful results of the intermarriage of near relations are appalling. It is impossible to gainsay these attested facts; yet there are numerous cases in which the children of such marriages are unusually brilliant in mind, and healthy in body.

How are we to account for such directly opposite results,—can kindred blood produce both good and evil? Doubtless, there are cases in which persons nearly related might marry, and no evil ensue; while in other instances the marriage of second cousins would produce diseased and idiotic children. All this may seem mysterious, but is, undoubtedly, the effect of fixed and unchanging laws.

The child is the blending, the further development of both parents; and if the two are alike in anything, their offspring will inherit that peculiarity in a still more exaggerated form. If then, there be a healthy mental activity, the child may excel; or if the functions were already excessively active in both parents, in the child it may be so undue as to become morbid, and altogether abnormal. The result, even in this good direction, may be a highly nervous tendency, insanity, or an early death.

Again, if the parents have each the same weakness, mental or physical, these will become still further developed in their descendants. The blind, the deaf and dumb, and the weak-minded, are the natural effects of such causes.

In the early ages of the world, among Greeks, Jews, and other nations, the marriage of half brothers and sisters was frequent. Such unions were, generally, less prolific, but the children were likely to be finely formed and beautiful. The same thing now, when the race is enfeebled by luxurious living, artificial habits, and inherited disease, would result in sterility, abortions, and idiotic monstrosities.

We see something of the old result produced by the union of cousins and other relations, among the society of friends, in some communities in our midst. The children become gentle, refined, and wonderfully alike; they may be recognized without their plain dress. These marriages are frequently without offspring; and if continued through several generations, produce the well-known disastrous consequences.

Consanguinity in itself may be no obstacle to a prosperous union; but similarity of temperament, or of organism, or of tendencies, is a most fearful obstacle in the present state of civilivation. Such similarity, although it may not manifest itself strongly, is almost certain to exist in blood relations; hence such unions should be discouraged. All possible moral considerations are arrayed against them.

In a country town in western New Jersey lived two cousins united in wedlock. They were large, portly persons of a lymphatic temperament, resembling each other in looks more than do most brothers and sisters. They had ten children; two were boys of ordinary ability, but all the others were idiotic. Most of them died early. Two daughters, however, lived to the age of womanhood; and the friend who gave me this fact said that they were mere lumps of flesh, helpless, and apparently soulless; yet strangely like their parents in form and feature. The father and mother were both healthy and intelligent, and outlived all of their ten children. After the wife's death the husband married again, and the children of this union, all of whom are still living, possess ordinary good health and intelligence.

Family weaknesses, or physical peculiarities, will descend through one parent from generation to generation, in despite of counteracting tendencies from the other. The trait, whatever it be, will frequently disappear in one generation to reappear in the next. Then if both parents possess it, it is certain to be greatly exaggerated in the descendants.

Are any husband and wife exceedingly nervous and irritable? Let them expect their children to be like themselves. Are they, one or both, restless, often sleepless, and "broken down in nervous system?" Let them anticipate for their children an afflicted life and an early death. In addition to all this, are they cousins?—entailing on their offspring a thousand nameless acute tendencies,—let them look forward to insanity, or some form of mental mania,—it is almost inevitable.

The forms of disease, both mental and physical, are so various that it is impossible to predicate fixed and certain results with any degree of accuracy. The causes acting are hidden and complicated, and our knowledge of modifying circumstances imperfect; yet we can lay down general laws, general effects, from general principles and causes.

Temperate habits and an enlightened education may do much to overcome even organic weaknesses. There are parents with feeble constitutions who, by conscientiously obeying the laws of health, steadily accumulate a new stock of vitality. These carry their children above their own level in mind and in body; they give them an upward tendency, and may reasonably expect a healthy offspring.

Another couple are healthy and hardy, but they live too fast,—they are gradually exhausting their strength and vitality; and their children are born below themselves. The impetus given them is in the descending grade,—they tend downward as the others tend upward. "What a mysterious dispensation," exclaims the devout fatalist, "these children of weakly parents are healthy, whilst those of the strong ones are feeble!"

CHAPTER FOURTH.

There is probably no trait or peculiarity of either mind or body, which has not, from time to time, been directly transmitted to children. The tendency to virtue and to vice, to genius and to dullness, to the genial easy enjoyment of life, and to the gloomiest hypochondria, has descended from parent to child for generation after generation; each family retaining its own peculiarities, physical, mental or moral, almost intact.

We often find most marked family idiosyncracies—most fantastic and ludicrous resemblances, looks and ways, which depend neither upon features nor complexion, and are recognised by a stranger more readily than by an acquaintance; but which we can all see arise more from a grouping of traits and qualities, than from any one peculiarity.

A friend related to me this fact; I give it as nearly as possible in her own words.

" When I was a school girl, I was sitting beside a companion, and taking her hand in mine, I was measuring it against my own palm; it was so broad that it astonished me; and good breeding could scarcely prevent me from uttering an exclamation of surprise.

"'It's large enough for the fifth finger,' said the girl, laughing good-naturedly. 'I like to have had it. My grandfather, my great-grandfather, and my great-great-grandfather had five fingers on the left hand. The extra one, which was small, was always cut off when the child was a baby; but it reappeared in the next generation. My father escaped, but I like to have inherited the family mark.'

"She held up her hand, and I could really fancy that another finger was ready to come out of the large joint at the base of the little finger, which was unusually long. I found this was no joke of the girl's, but a literal fact. Her father was a Methodist minister then living in Ohio; and I afterwards spent a week in her family, where I heard the story of the hereditary five fingers repeated, and solemnly attested by others of the family."

Deafness is very often transmitted to children. I have known two cases where the mother, and nearly every child was "hard of hearing;" and other cases where the infirmity was inherited from the father, or from one of the grand-parents. There was no more room to doubt that it was inherited, than there is to doubt that the pug nose, the coarse black hair, or high cheek bones are hereditary when they are the fac-similes of the parents. Yet one child in a family may have black hair, while another's is light, fine, and curly. Nature seems capricious, though she is really most orderly, staid, and law-abiding in all her ways. Her resources are so numerous, that she draws from various, and sometimes most unexpected and unacknowledged, (such as the mother's imagination) sources, to produce her results. We are puzzled, and ready to doubt or to deny their legitimacy; yet, by discarding time-worn errors and ignorant prejudices, and allowing ourselves a wider range of observation, and a more careful watchfulness, we shall learn that this is folly.

"There was a proud family of D————s, and another of W————s, living in Eastern Massachusetts," said an old gentleman of seventy-five, " who had intermarried ever since they came into the country, and before for aught I know. They were all cousins and double cousins; at last things came to such a pass that there was hardly a sound child born among them. They were blind, or deaf and dumb, or foolish; or something else was the matter, till it became a country talk, and every body said that it was because they married blood-relations. They had to give it up, and marry other people; and when I went back there a few years ago, both names had run out. There were no D————s or W————s as far as I could learn, in the community. It might have been cousins marrying —I don't know about that; I know people said so.— But I have known cousins to marry, and they had healthy, bright children."

This old gentleman's testimony seemed to me just in point; he had no theory to maintain, and merely stated a fact in reply to a question.

If any defect existed on the father's side, and the children of brothers were to marry, this defect would be very likely to be exaggerated in their offspring; while if the son should marry his mother's niece, though she were his own cousin, yet that particular defect would be less likely to appear in their children.

Its recurrence would be still less probable if his wife were in no wise related; their opposite qualities would modify and limit each other; and they might, under ordinary circumstances, reasonably expect a proper and well developed offspring. One who marries a relation, must always do it at a risk; he and his children may escape, and yet the sin be visited upon the third and the fourth generations.

"The transmission of any infirmity," says Dr. Howe, "is not always direct. It is not always in the same form. It may be modified by the influence of one sound parent; it may skip one generation; it may affect one in one form, and another in another; so in a thousand ways, it may elude observation, because it may affect a child merely by *diminishing*, not by destroying the vigor of his mind and body—almost paralyzing one mental faculty, or giving fearful activity to one animal propensity, and so reappearing in the child in a different dress from that it wore in the parents. Variety is the great law of Nature, and it holds good in the transmission of diseased tendencies, as well as in every thing else. But unerring certainty, too, is alike characteristic of this law, and let no one flatter himself or herself that its penalty can be evaded."

A Committee in Massachusetts reported to the Senate upon the cases of seventeen families, in which there were marriages of blood-relations. This is the statement. "Most of the parents were intemperate or scrofulous; some were both the one and the other; of course there were other causes to increase the chances of infirm offspring, besides that of the intermarriage.

There were born unto them *ninety-five* children, of whom FORTY-FOUR were idiotic, twelve others were scrofulous and puny, one was deaf, and one was a dwarf! In some cases, all the children were either very scrofulous or puny. In one family of eight children, five were idiotic."

Thus Nature inflicts her penalties for all violations of her laws. Her processes are often slow and unseen—but the results sure. Our safety lies in studying carefully her ways, and ruling ourselves by her precepts; when we are ignorant or in doubt, let us err on the side of caution.

The witty "Professor" of the Atlantic Monthly says, "It is frightful to be in an atmosphere of family idiosyncracies; to see all the hereditary uncomeliness or infirmity of body, all the defects of speech, all the failings of temper, intensified by concentration, so that every fault of our own finds itself multiplied by reflections, like our images in a saloon lined by mirrors!—Nature knows what she is about. The centrifugal principle which grows out of the antipathy of like to like, is only the repetition in character of the arrangement we see expressed materially in certain seed-capsules, which burst and throw the seed to all points of the compass. A house is a large pod with a human germ or two in each of its cells or chambers; it opens by dehescence of the front door by and by, and projects one of its germs into Kansas, another to San Francisco, another to Chicago, and so on; and this that Smith may not be Smithed to death, and Brown be Browned into a mad-house, but mix in with the world again, and struggle back to average humanity."

Truly, Nature understands her work, and she will do her best to see that it is properly executed. Yet she needs our co-operation as sensible and reflective beings, to aid her in carrying out her designs. If we will not aid her as moral beings, she will leave the Cain's mark upon our children and our children's children; thus through them—through their trials and sufferings, will she teach us how holy and equitable are her laws; since, to violate them brings ruin not only to ourselves, but to those dearer than self—the children of our love. There is nothing more touching—more reproving, than the anguish which comes to the parent through the defects of his child—defects visited upon the innocent through the faults of the guilty!

CHAPTER FIFTH.

The laws of Nature are the principles which inhere in Nature. They are the attributes or the essential qualities of things ; and are necessarily, as permanent and indestructible as are the existences to which they belong. Natural laws are not only a part of Nature, but they are its only vital and permanent forces. They are the exponents of that activity within it which saves it from stagnation.

Of course, then, these innate controlling principles, the only real or Natural laws, must be always operative—always tending to like results under like circumstances.

We have only to study the principles of organized matter, and then to clasify the knowledge obtained, in order to predicate facts, and to make deductions which shall be the same in every given instance. If we have tested the properties of one specimen of pure iron and have analyzed one ray of sunshine we understand thus much of all iron, and of all sunlight. So of each principle in Nature ; whether in the physical, mental, or moral departments. If we have discovered any essential law, either of matter or of mind it is a law which is always operative, always if left undisturbed, certain to produce the same results; and always if disturbed, seeking according to its intrinsic nature, to overcome the disturbance by exerting its force towards the normal and desired end.

Probably no nation has surpassed the French in a close observation of the laws of Nature; and in a philosophical induction and classification of its results.

"All successful men," says Emerson, "have agreed in one thing; they were *causationists*. They believed that things went not by luck, but by law; that there was not a weak or cracked link in the chain that joins the first and the last of things. A belief in causality or strict connexion between every trifle and the principle of living, and in consequence, belief in compensation, or that nothing is got for nothing — characterizes all valuable minds, and must control every effort that is made by an industrious one."

Geoffroy Saint Hilaire made the study of monstrosities a speciality. I have translated the following summary of the fruits of that study, from a memoir by his son, recently published in Paris.

Up to the time when Meckel and Geffroy St. Hilaire began to reduce the chaos of observation, hypothesis and fiction, relating to monstrosities into something like the order of science, the strange anomalies which were frequently presenting themselves, both in human beings and in animals, were considered, first,—as inexplicable "freaks of Nature;" second,—as the result of pre-existent deformities; third,—as irregularities inexplicable and irreducible to law. The very term monstrosity implies a contradiction to all laws. And for a philosopher to have said to the world,—This monstrosity is the product of precisely the same laws as those which produce the normal being; would have been to draw upon himself something of the wonderment and scorn which rise in the mind, when first men are told that social and historical phenomena capricious and wayward as they appear, are serial products of laws absolute and ascertainable. What Comte has done for sociology, Geoffroy did for teratology. He considers monstrosities as organic deviations. They are not the product of hazard or caprice. They have their laws; these laws are the same as those that form all organisms; instead of escaping the general laws of organization, they only serve to prove their universality.

Geoffroy Saint Hilaire studies the circumstances attending the birth of monsters, and he sees in a great number of cases an accident; for instance, a fall, a blow, a lively moral impression, disturb a pregnancy, until then regular, which from that moment becomes difficult, sickly, extraordinary and terminates at nine, eight, or seven months in the birth of a monster. Still more, he goes so far as to discern, at least in regard to pseudocephalic, and acephalic monsters, the nature, and above all, at what period the accident took place which caused them.

The certainty of his diagnosis is such that more than once he dares affirm upon the circumstances of the pregnancy, or of the birth, that which the mother herself had denied; but which she saw herself compelled to avow. " Who has revealed to you our secret?"

One day a physician told him he was about to present to the Academy an acephalous monster. "Will you at the same time present the twin first born and their common placenta?" asked Geoffroy. "Ah!" replied the astonished physician, "have you then seen it?" "I only know what you have just told me."

From the observation of the circumstances which caused the malformations, Saint Hiliare passes to that of monsters themselves, and from the determination of the immediate causes to those more remote. There is, according to him, in many cases, an adhesion established with the young embryo, between one or several of its organs and the membranes of the egg, or of the placenta.

When a mother in the first period of gestation receives a violent shock, either mental or physical, it produces a quick and forcible contraction of the whole muscular system, including the uterus. When the fœtal membrane receives this shock, it contracts suddenly; the result is a slight laceration; two phenomena then follow, viz., the flowing of a part of the ammiotic-water, and the union of the torn ends of the filament of the membrane, with the contiguous parts of the body of the embryo; hence are formed fibres of adhesion, whose presence, sometimes temporarily, sometimes permanently, disturb more or less seriously the development of the embryo; either because they retain the organs out of their natural cavities, or that they oppose the reunions which would otherwise have taken place; or that they delay, or even prevent the formation of the parts which ought ultimately to appear.

In 1826 a vast incubating establishment having been formed at Auteuil, he recommenced his experiments on a grand scale, and varied them in a thousand ways. They consisted in hatching eggs, placed at first in all respects under ordinary circumstances. Then at the end of a certain lapse of time—three days at most differently modified; for instance, shaken more or less violently, perforated in different places; but above all, maintained in a vertical position, either on the small or the large end; or half of the surface well covered with a layer of wax or varnish that would render the shell air-tight.

The results of these experiments entirely fulfilled the expectations of the author. Neither among the chickens which were hatched, nor among the fœtus which died before hatching, were there found any double monsters. On the contrary, there were obtained a number, relatively very considerable, of organic deviations; some constituting simple hémitéries, others very complex anomalies, monsters differing in nothing from those which Nature presents spontaneously to our observation in animals and in man himself.

These experiments, several times repeated, have always had the same results, viz., that embryos which placed under ordinary circumstances, would have been naturally developed—which even had commenced to develope themselves naturally, have become, their development being interrupted, anomalous, monstrous even. Anomalies, therefore, do not exist previous to fecundation; *but are the results of a disturbance happening in the course of the development of embryos at first perfectly regular.*

The study of monstrosities, continues Saint Hiliare, which, according to the ideas of the ancients, could only satisfy a vain curiosity, is now invested with a scientific character, and takes its place by the side of normal beings.

The organization of monsters is subject to rules and to laws, and those laws are but the general laws of organization.

I admit no more a special physiology for cases of vicious organization than a special philosophy to account for some facts isolated, and left without explanation. There is monstrosity, but not a deviation from ordinary laws.*

To the question of what is a monster? Science answered still at the commencement of this century— "A freak of Nature; a being created without any rule, and in the absence of any end;" and philosophers thought it possible to add, " It is a specimen of those laws of chance which, according to Atheists, must have given birth to the Universe; God has permitted them in order to show us what creation is without Him."†

Anatomical philosophy, on the contrary, replies, "Monsters are not freaks of Nature; their organization is subjected to rules rigorously determined, and these

---

* I could quote any amount of cases from the works of Saint Hilaire to substantiate the preceding opinion, if the subject were not of so painful, and so disagreeable a nature. Those who have any doubts as to the correctness of this author's views, can consult his works in several quarto volumes, illustrated, in the Astor Library.

† Expressions of Chateaubriand in his Genius of Christianity.

are identical with those which govern the normal beings."

A monster is a being in whom are not accomplished the transformations which should elevate it successively to its normal type,—a being which has met with a hindrance, or a delay of its development, and has remained in some respects an embryo,—as if Nature had stood still in order to give to our too slow observation the time and the means to overtake her.

Monstrosity is not, therefore, the result of a blind chance; but rather the product of a disturbed action of the same beneficent laws of Nature which secure health and fair proportions when allowed to conclude their functions without disturbance.

The preceding facts and illustrations will account equally well for the production of idiocy and imbecility, as for malformations. The two former are as certainly caused by a disturbed gestation as the latter. Hence no mother will hereafter be permitted to say, pointing to her idiotic child, "behold! the afflicted of God," for science may ask her the question, "How did this thing occur, by what unfortunate accident, or didst thou dare to lay impious hands on and mar that which God in His wisdom and goodness intended should be perfect?"

Surely, if a knowledge of this subject were to become more general, idiocy, imbecility, insanity, and unbalanced mental organizations would be less common. No subject that has hitherto engaged the attention of the philanthropist, or the political economist, can compare with this, for it is the basis of all human progress.

CHAPTER SIXTH.

It is substantiated beyond a doubt, that attempted abortion is a frequent cause of imbecility. It is always difficult to prove a fact like this—few mothers will willingly make confession of such a crime; but by some specious sophistry, will endeavor to hide it even from themselves. I have, however, obtained the testimony, published and unpublished, of several distinguished names, like those of Dr. Howe, of Boston, and J. B. Richards of New York, and others, who have given years to the investigation of the various causes of idiocy, and they are all unanimous in their testimony on this point. Several cases are given by Dr. Howe, in which young women attempted to conceal the unborn proofs of shame; but failing in this, they are married, and the child is idiotic; though all children born afterwards of the same parents are sound and healthy. One woman had seven sound children, and another had six born in wedlock; although the oldest child of each of them, upon whom abortion had been attempted, was idiotic."

Other cases are given where mothers have had from four to eight healthy children each, and afterwards they had from one to four, who were idiotic—made so by attempted abortions, because the mothers thought they had children enough. Out of four hundred idiots examined by a committee in Massachusetts, seven were known to have resulted from this cause; and the presumptive evidence of the same cause was very strong in many other instances.

The following fact was given to me by a friend, in whose veracity I have the most implicit confidence.

The mother of several fine healthy children, who thought that the number was already large enough, attempted to destroy the embryo life of another expected one; she did not succeed, but the powerful medicine which she had taken enfeebled the child both in mind and body. He was the last, the weakest and frailest of all the family. While the older brothers were sent to school, to college, and are becoming men of mark, this weak-minded son had to be educated in a private institution in the country, to save the family credit—and will always be incompetent to take care of himself.

Behold a cause for a life-long sorrow to this wretched mother, when she contemplates the wreck of manhood presented by her youngest born, and contrasts his blighted condition with that of her older sons, who are in full possession of all the blessings that vigorous health, high culture, and success in life can bestow.

How many truly logical theories would seem at a first glance to be refuted by an example like this!— The parents at his birth were in the full vigor of health and maturity. According to all physiological and psychological laws, it would seem that he should have been among the most vigorous of his family, both in mind and body.

We will suppose an elder sister to be reflecting upon the subject of transmitted tendencies: In this instance it would seem to her that she herself, the child of the immature and early youth of both parents, was much the superior of the child of their hardy middle life. Thus, judging from this deceptive case, she might lose faith in all theories upon this most important subject. "Do I not see," she would exclaim "that it is all a chance—that nothing can be determined about these matters—that one child is healthy and intelligent, and another feeble and stupid, and yet we can assign no cause for this? Why need one be haunted with the constant feeling that every wrong or mistaken thing that is done may produce evil effects upon future children? The thought is a nightmare, and I will throw it off! When I do wrong I will suffer willingly, but I could not endure the thought that poor little children might be life-long sufferers for my faults."

Thus this poor girl will be less careful of her health—her temper—of all her ways, than she otherwise might have been. Many a one has been tempted upon the plea of bearing the penalty of his own wrong doing, to sacrifice future good to present indulgence. Let such feel that they cannot suffer alone—that the whole human family are bound together, and that innocent ones must share with them the consequences of evil doing.

The natural laws appertaining to humanity are simple; but they are all interlinked and complicated with each other, and although the exact result may not be predicated by any finite mind, yet we know that all violations of them are visited with their legitimate consequences. We must learn to look far and carefully for our data, before we come to conclusions adverse to the wisdom and goodness of a beneficent Creator.

I know of no better thought to suggest to one that is tempted to a like crime with this unfortunate mother, than that spoken by a friend, to a young wife not long since. She found herself enceinte at a time which was particularly unsatisfactory to her, as she had just planned a journey of some months to be spent abroad with her husband. The result was that she had to remain at home while her husband went alone. "I wish I had taken something at first," said the young wife in her loneliness. "I would have done so at the time, but my husband would not hear of it." "Yes," said the friend, "and when your son has grown to manhood, tell him that you wanted to kill him, and that you were sorry afterwards you had not done so—but his father would not let you!"

It can only be from a want of reflection on this subject that so few persons look upon this fearful crime as murder.

A prominent lawyer in a neighboring State was engaged in trying a case of great importance. It had occupied his time and thoughts for many days and nights, and deprived him of his natural rest. To his great joy he gained the suit, but found himself at the close completely prostrated both in mind and body. He felt that he required repose, but necessity compelled him to return home at once. Exhausted as he was, he set out immediately in a lumbering stage-coach, traveled night and day without rest, many hundred miles, over bad and sometimes rough and mountainous roads, ending his journey with a long ride on horseback. He thus traversed nearly the length of a large and mountainous State, by these most primitive methods, and arrived at home late one evening, after an unusually long absence.

The following is his own testimony in regard to the evil consequences which resulted from this infringement of the organic laws of his being. "There is not a doubt in my mind that our idiot child was conceived that night, after my return home in a state of physical and mental exhaustion."

No other cause could be suggested, either by himself or his wife, for this terrible affliction. Their other children were bright and intelligent; but this one was hopelessly idiotic.

The vitality of the father was exhausted, and he bequeathed his own prostrate condition to the new embryo life. This fact proves much in regard to the father's influence in planting the new germ of existence. It proves, also, that man cannot violate the laws of life and health, and yet expect to beget sound offspring.

Here is another case in point.

A young New England couple began life together as industrious and well-to-do farmers. They were both robust in health, cheerful in disposition, and remarkably well adapted to each other. Not being too much alike in temperament and organization, they were reasonably entitled to expect a fine offspring. All the conditions were unusually favorable to this end; their first child fully realized their highest expectations, and was from the first unusually bright and attractive.

After the birth of this child, owing to causes not necessary to state, the father became suddenly and deplorably intemperate. When a respectable New Englander gives up his character and good name to become a sot, his case is desperate. The higher his former estate, the lower he is likely to fall,—goaded on as he is, by shame and remorse.

This man became the lowest of his class,—his property squandered, his family beggared. In this state of affairs a second child was born to him,—it was idiotic; its head was small, but well formed. This was regarded by those who investigated the case, as a marked illustration of arrested development. The head was no larger than that of a fœtus of a few months.

This sad event added to the unhappy state of mind of the father, whose habits continued from bad to worse. In time they had a third child born,—also an idiot; its head was both small and malformed. The father, who was, after all, a man at heart, was present at its birth, and when he saw its blighted condition, gave way to a paroxysm of anguish and despair, and wept aloud. Friends sought to comfort him. "I will never be the father of another idiot," he exclaimed, as he rushed from the house. After a short time he returned, and exclaimed, "Wife, give me your hand, I have signed the pledge,—I will never take another drop of strong drink." He kept his promise. Their position as a family from that day was upward, until they were again in comfortable and respectable circumstances. The fourth child, born during this second period of prosperity, was bright and active, although not equal in intellect to the first.

A fact like this should speak for itself. It was related to me by one who was himself the teacher of these unfortunate children, when they were inmates of a private institution for idiots, over which he presided.* He has been more than twelve years engaged in this work of benevolence, and has spent much time in investigating the causes which lead to mental imbecility.

He believes in this case, that the mother's thoughts and sympathies were following the father; that they were absent from herself and from the child, and thus the proper developement of the fœtus was impeded ; that in the first instance it was arrested a few months after conception, and in the second it was abnormal from the begining. He studied attentively all the symptoms of the children, and compared them with the facts of the case, thus carefully arriving at his conclusions. In many instances Mr. Richards has been able to ascertain the causes of the imbecility by merely watching the peculiarities of the different cases which have come under his notice, and in every instance, he has found by subsequent inquiry, his inferences were correct.

Mr. Richards had under his charge at different times,

---

* James B. Richards.

four idiotic children of a family who resided in one of the Southern States. He had frequently endeavored by interrogating the parents, to ascertain the cause or causes of this unparallelled affliction; but without success until he overheard the following conversation between his wife and the old colored nurse who accompanied the fourth child.

"If Missis please, I's like to speak to her 'bout dis child."

"You had better speak to Mr. Richards if anything is the matter with him."

"No, no, de men don't know so much as de women 'bout children. I's hear de minister and de doctor talk 'nough 'bout dese things to satisfy me on dat subject. You see, missis, dis child's got no soul, or if he has, 'tis so prisoned up in dis little head it can't get out; so I can't 'muse myself wid talking to him like any other child; den I's got noffin' else to think 'bout but ponder and wonder why dis child's made so foolish and good for nuffin'. 'Spose missis Richards know so much 'bout children, she'll tell me?"

"That subject has puzzled wiser heads than yours or mine, aunty. But if you think women knew more than men about it, why did you not ask your mistress?"

"I did. She say just like de minister, 'It please de Lord to make 'em so.'"

"Were you not satisfied with that answer?"

"No, mem!"

"Why not?"

"Because it did not please de Lord to make de four

first children of my missis like dis one, so soft and limp; dey's got plenty back-bone, plenty brain."

"If you have thought so much about these things, tell me now what you think caused the difference be-between the first and last four of your mistress' children?"

"Sometimes I think one thing, sometimes another. When my missis first married she have children all regular, one after another all right; den she say she hab no more, she want to trabel an' 'joy herself, so she hab no more for long time; den she begin again; when de first foolish child come, I's think 'twas sent to punish my mas'r, 'cause he sell my oldest gal down to Orleans, after I's beg an' pray him jest let me keep her one year more; but when he strike me and sell my child to de bad white man, I's pray to de Lord to smite him with de rod of iron; to punish him trough his children. So when de first idiot child came, I think de Lord heard my supplication; 'cause my mas'r took away my child, He give him dis punishment. Well, after while I got over my bad feeling t'wards my mas'r and prayed de good Lord to take off de curse, and gib de next child his soul; but 'twas no use, tree more come all foolish. So den I first begin to tink what for made 'em so."

"Well, what did you think next was the cause?"

"Now dat's what I's want to ask Missis Richards 'bout. 'Spose when my missis no want to have any more; 'spose de Lord to punish her, make 'em like dis one?"

"No, indeed! or half of the children born would be idiotic."

"Well, den, 'spose my missis take someting or do someting not to have 'em come, 'spose dat would spile 'em so?"

"What put such a thought in your head, aunty?"

"Why I's troubled 'bout dis ting,—I's feared 'twas de curse I put on mas'r 'bout my gal. As I's telling my Jim how thinking 'bout it, kept me 'wake nights. He say you come wid me to de cotton field, I'll show you how de Lord 'ranges dese tings. So he tell me to look at de rows of hills, some coming up all right, some no come up at all. What for, says he, you s'pose da no all come up? Cause I'se cursed 'em? No such ting; I's planted a hard sun-baked clod of dirt on de seed. Cause when de driver say, you Jim, hoe so many rows of hills afore supper time; now if da no all come up, den I's no got 'em all to hoe! So you just neber trouble yoursel' 'bout dat curse. De Lord's not so unjust as to take away children's souls, cause you pray Him to punish dar fader."

At this point, Mr. Richards thought it prudent to interrupt the conversation; hence the sagacious reader is left to draw his own inferences.

In closing this chapter, which has been made thus long by an earnest conviction of the importance of the subject, it seems necessary to impress upon woman, as primarily the most important agent, in the transmission of good or evil qualities, the great responsibilities which rest upon her maternal condition. Let every mother so educate her daughters for maternity that they may escape the dread evils of which this chapter treats, —let not a false delicacy prevent her from keeping such knowledge from them,—let her so enlighten and elevate their moral sentiments, that they shall exhibit in the beauty of their lives the reflex action of the principles she has inculcated. If the mother possesses any desirable talent, or any beautiful quality of heart, let her so exercise that talent, and cultivate that quality that it may bloom in greater brilliancy in her children and in her children's children. So if there should exist among the subtleties of her own character, any dark spot, let her exert all her moral strength in order to eradicate it, that its shadow may not darken the third generation. Let her surround the growing soul with all good influcies,—let her cultivate all noble impulses, all holy aspirations,—let her breathe into the opening flower, by the magic power of a mother's love, such knowledge as shall prepare it for the world in all its antagonisms, and all its agreements,—so shall she see in the final fruit an ample reward for all her care, her self-denial, and her self-abnegation. Finally, let all those, to whom these suggestions may come, lay them closely to their hearts, and seek to embody in their lives the principles they present,—founded as they are upon laws as fixed and immutable as the power of the Almighty, and as beneficial as His mercy. By these means countless souls will have been made sinless, and the trust which God hath placed in our hands, and the inheritance which has come to us from the past, will be bequeathed to the future, with added purity, and with brighter lustre.

CHAPTER SEVENTH.

A REMARKABLE case of malformation caused by the imagination of the mother, was related to me by a member of the family in which it occurred.

A young lady whose mental accomplishments, personal graces, wealth, and social position commanded the attention of the noblest of the other sex, became attached to a young gentleman every way her equal, and was engaged to be married. Owing to an accident which occurred in his childhood, her betrothed was lame. One day a married sister, in a moment of levity mimicked him, limping up and down the room. "See, this is the way you will have to go through life with your husband, dot and carry one!" cried she gaily.

The young girl grieved and distressed by this unfeeling ridicule, burst into tears, bravely affirming that the lameness of her intended only made him more dear to her; it was not a moral defect that it should be visited with obloquy; but it merited instead, the most cordial sympathy and respect. The other, remorseful, and softened by her distress, earnestly besought forgiveness. Thus an agitating scene transpired which resulted most unfortunately for the married sister, who was within a few months of her confinement,—at birth, one limb of the child was soft and flexible apparently wanting in the bony formation; but the attending physician thought this of little consequence,—bone would soon form and no evil result would follow. The proper ossification did ensue, but so tardily that, from neglect or inattention, the limb became crooked and shorter than the other. Hence another cripple for life—another victim of maternal indiscretion,—or rather ignorance of the laws and the duties of parent-hood.

There are many facts in Nature which it is impossible to gainsay, yet we cannot tell *why* they are thus, nor yet *how* they are produced. The law of all things is, indeed, Nature's universal mystery. How, in the dark recesses of the earth, is the diamond formed— whence its bright scintillations? What gives to the crystal its geometrical lines—its positive and negative poles?* How does the grass grow? How does each seed produce its own plant, flower, and fruit, each after its kind? How does the human spirit modify its physical frame; and how is it modified in turn by the peculiarities of its organism? When we can answer these and myriads of other unsolved problems, then we may resolve the mystery of the mother's mental impressions as affecting the welfare of her unborn child. Meantime, if we are to place any reliance upon human testimony, or upon our own observation, w must credit facts like the above. Notwithstanding the doctors often ignore such cases, dozens of them may

---

* Rachenbach's Dynamics of Magnetism.

be heard of in any gathering of matrons, whether in a tenement-house parlor, or at a fashionable watering-place, whenever the subject chances to come up for consideration.

Fact before theory is a rule of the majority. Yet the mere gathering of facts would be an unprofitable occupation, if we could not also trace from them the laws or principles by which they were produced; and thereby multiply them if desirable, or avoid them if objectionable.

The scientific have been known to torture fact to make it harmonize with theory. "I have heard," says Foudillac, "of a philosopher who had had the happiness of thinking that he had discovered a principle which was to explain all the wonderful phenomena of chemistry, and who, in the ardor of his self-gratulation, hastened to communicate his discovery to a skillful chemist. The chemist had the kindness to listen to him, and then calmly told him that there was but one unfortunate circumstance for his discovery, that the chemical facts were precisely the converse of what he supposed them to be. "Well, then," said the philosopher, "have the goodness to tell me what they are, that I may explain them on my system."*

A case of a similar nature to the preceding was related to me by the wife of a Presbyterian minister from one of the Eastern States. Her youngest sister, a gentle, tender-hearted girl, soon after her marriage accompanied her husband to New Orleans, where he was engaged in business. They resided in the imme-

---

* Discourses of Sir William Hamilton, p. 50.

diate neighborhood of a French creole woman who was in the habit of whipping her female slaves almost daily. At such times the poor creatures would beg most piteously for mercy, and fill the air with their painful cries. The sympathy of the tenderly-reared New England girl was so agonized by this barbarous cruelty, that she used frequently to stop her ears with her fingers, in order to shut out the screams. Her first child, born under such influences, was so bright and sensitive that she was nearly two years of age before her parents discovered that she was entirely deaf. The poor stricken mother went almost frantic with grief when the affliction of her child was forced upon her conviction. She at once recognized the cause; and attributed it to the suffering she endured while endeavoring to close her ears against the cries of the poor slave women.

Such facts show how extremely susceptible some women are during the period of gestation; and also how important it is to guard them from all painful emotions or unpleasant influences at that particular time.

In a small company of matrons, on one occasion, this subject came under discussion. Several very remarkable cases of moral obliquity were narrated, with the causes which produced them; many, also, similar to the preceding,—and some malformations not unlike those found in the works of Geoffroy Saint Hilaire. An elderly lady present said she knew a perfect safeguard against sudden frights, or any untoward events at that critical period,—which was, first, to think of your situation—that effort persisted in would repel all evil influences—second, endeavor to divert your mind, or change your thoughts, by an agreeable book, active occupation, or cheerful company.

Many of the laws of human nature, not put down in the books, were discussed on that occasion, from the woman's stand-point, from which, owing to the nature of the subject, the view should be more clear and comprehensive than any other. This little band of earnest mothers, keenly observant, eager for knowledge, ready to sacrifice every selfish desire, or present enjoyment, in order to insure the future well-being of their children, were only a type of their sex. Perhaps the millennium will be near at hand when fathers begin to be as ambitious of leaving worthy descendants behind them when they die, as large estates.

3*

CHAPTER EIGHTH.

I MIGHT adduce fact after fact to show that the child of parents over-wrought must inherit an enfeebled constitution.* This violation of one of the organic laws of life is frequently followed by a transmitted tendency to some of the protean forms of scrofula; or if actual disease is not present, the organs are so frail and inactive as to be unable to resist the ordinary diseases of childhood, and thus the poor victim becomes a life-long sufferer, or is hurried to an early grave.

During the first part of this century scrofula was much more common than at a later period. It was usually called the king's evil, and considered incurable. So recently as 1840 a work on this disease was published by a French physician, in which it was stated that tuberculous scrofula was congenital, and always inherited; and if it appeared in one child of a family, it was certain to be latent, and would sooner or later develope itself in the systems of all the others. If it did not attack the glands of the neck or face in the ordinary way, it was sure to manifest itself by tubercles in the lungs or some other organs, or by

* See Appendix B.

tumors in the abdominal viscera, either of which must ultimately prove fatal.

Impressed with the apparent truth and importance of the knowledge contained in this book, I spoke of it to a friend who had a daughter afflicted with this dire disease, in order to caution her in regard to her other children. She assured me that she was under no apprehension on account of her younger children, for scrofula was not hereditary in either her husband's or her own family; and that she did not look upon the affliction of her eldest daughter as a disease, but rather an indication of a weak and inactive organization. She said, also, that the life of suffering and prospective early death of this ill-fated child overshadowed her conscience with a dark cloud, from which there was no escape. True, she had sinned ignorantly, but that reflection could not palliate the anguish of mind she experienced when she contrasted the blighted condition of this patient angelic child, with that of her younger sisters, who, blessed with health and fair symmetrical forms, enjoyed life and youth with the keenest zest.

"My husband," she continued, "soon after our marriage, having become dissatisfied with the vicissitudes of a mercantile life, exchanged some property in the metropolis for a place in the country; where he hoped to enjoy a tranquil life, to indulge his literary tastes, and his love for rural pursuits. Our home was situated on one of the most picturesque branches of the noble Hudson; was susceptible of much improvement, both in regard to its natural beauties, and its remunerating resources. My husband being some twenty years my senior, and fond of sedentary habits, allowed me to take the management of affairs, both in-doors and out. So, being ambitious and energetic, and possessing a passionate love for beautiful trees, I planned many improvements, but in endeavoring to carry them out, I overtaxed my strength, and my children suffered the penalty. My first, a son, was prematurely born, at seven months, with only vitality enough to survive a few hours. That the loss of this child was caused by over-exertion on my part, I was well aware; yet this state of affairs seemed to be the fatal necessity of my position. Subjected to raids of visitors from the neighboring city at all seasons, with insufficient domestic help, each day and hour bringing its imperative labor, not to be evaded by an orderly housekeeper, I thought I could only submit for the present, and hope for more harmonious arrangements in the future. So things went on in the usual way another year, when I again became a mother. This event occurred at a time when improvements were being made on the place, which required many hands, who had to be provided for in the family. Domestic service not to be had at all times in the country, I was again at a critical period, subjected to exhausting fatigue. My second child was born at the full time, but in what the doctor called a heat, which so enfeebled her constitution that she did not walk alone until two years of age; I used to watch over her with fear and trembling—on so frail a tenure seemed to hang her existence. Notwithstanding the popular belief at that time—that if a child be born feeble or imperfect, it was the will of God—the conviction was impressed upon my mind that I was culpable, that I was the cause of this prostrated condition of my darling child. I then formed a resolution to persistently put from me the necessity which could work such cruel results to my children. How well I kept that resolve, the healthy constitutions and the beautifully developed forms of my youngest daughters will bear witness."

Consumption, also, when not hereditary, may frequently be traced to the same cause as that of the preceding fact. I know a healthy, but hard-working farmer and his wife, who, without any predisposition to lung complaints themselves, have lost seven of their ten children by consumption; while two of the survivors are in advanced stages of sure decline. This mother never rested. She worked up to the last moment before confinement; yet for more than twenty years of her life there never was three months at a time in which she was not either enceinte or nursing an infant. Their eldest child, a daughter, is still a healthy, robust woman, with a large and well-developed physical system. Such facts speak volumes. The only way of accounting for them is by supposing that the energies of both parents in this case were exhausted by excessive labor,—but that the eldest child, born while their constitutions were still young and vigorous,— escaped the family curse.

Excessive mental activity is often equally fatal in its effects upon offspring. Indeed, when carried to an extreme, it is even more disastrous; and has been known to result in hopeless idiocy. Here is a case in point.

A young lady who had exhausted her strength by study, teaching and various literary pursuits, while in a state of debility was married to a clergyman of congenial tastes and similar condition. This event became a new mental stimulant. They read and wrote together continually; so fascinated by the pleasures of this delightful intellectual companionship as seemingly to have risen above all weakness of the flesh. But Nature never allows herself to be overreached. If her laws are outraged, she is constrained to enforce her penalties,—their first child, born within a year of their marriage, was an idiot. The stricken parents, awakened to a sense of their responsibility by this sad event, began diligently to study and to obey the laws of both mind and body; and now arrived at middle life, they have a fine family of promising young children.

Women are generally more inclined to mental indolence than to intellectual activity. This is owing, probably, to the inferior mental discipline which is exacted from them in the course of their education. Yet examples are not wanting in which the irrepressible activity of the mother's mind during the period of gestation has produced precocious children; to whom this undue use of the mental faculties, if accompanied by a neglect of the laws of health, is highly detrimental. Although such children may have inherited a fine nervous temperament, and a large development of brain, unless sustained by a good physique, they are almost surely destined to an early grave; or if they live, their brilliant powers appear to burn themselves out, and they grow up common place persons. They had inherited no unnatural powers, it was only the premature development of an ordinary mind, and like the hot-house flowers, brought forward by artificial methods, they were the first to fade.

Cause and effect is Nature's universal law. All defective organism is traceable to causes; and is frequently the penalty paid by parents for laws which they have broken, and visited on the children, even to the third and the fourth generation. Thus does the Creator teach us, that the most valuable inheritance we can transmit to offspring, is a sound constitution,—the reward of a virtuous life: and also, that we are social beings, and that no man can live to himself only.

CHAPTER NINTH.

A LARGE portion of the time and efforts of the author in the present volume has been devoted to showing how the habits of the parents, whether good or bad, fasten their consequences upon the children. Nay, more than this, that each progenitor seems, as it were, to vaccinate his yet unborn descendants with the virus of his own nature; so that the child must take his tastes, tendencies and propensities, with more or less intensity according to circumstances, by natural indoctrination. If this be so, it is doubly important that there should be "mens sana in corpore sano," not only for the individual but for the race.*

It is becoming an accepted tenet of latter-day faith that all suffering is abnormal,—that it always involves

---

* The principal occupation of one of the large sea-port towns of New England was formerly fitting out whale-ships for the Pacific. The young men belonging to these vessels, after an absence of two or three years, returned home with constitutions impaired by exposure and salt provisions at sea. but still more by improper and injurious connections on shore. In consequence of these infringements of the laws of life and health, their descendants to the third and fourth generations of the present day, are suffering the penalty through diseases arising from inherited weaknesses and impurities.

guilt, either on the part of the sufferer, or of some ancestor, who has, by disregarding the laws of life and health, drawn down evil upon the head of the innocent. Many, indeed, sin through ignorance on this subject. It is, however, beginning to be understood that mankind are, in part at least, responsible for their ignorance, and that Nature and her Author do not forgive the unwitting offendor by preventing the painful consequences of his acts. That this is a part of the unchanging economy of Providence may be inferred from the evidences of Divine wisdom by which we are everywhere surrounded.

Weakness and feebleness, of whatever character, are therefore reprehensible, and should be combatted and overcome by persistent and vigorous efforts. We should teach every one that weakness is a disgrace, whether it be of mind or of body; that it reflects upon the parents, upon society, and upon the individual. Thus will they be made to feel their own responsibility, and to learn by what tenure life and health can be preserved.

While business and professional men like galley-slaves are chained to counting-rooms and offices, and their wives like Circassian slaves, are shut up in their houses in Egyptian darkness all summer and worse than Egyptian heat all winter, to make them look delicately beautiful, we must expect fearful bills of infant mortality, and frightful evidences of early decline. The public thought is broader on this subject now than formerly; yet so perverted are the tastes of some persons that delicacy of constitution is considered a badge of aristocracy, and the daughters would feel themselves depreciated by too robust health ; the mothers, also, would look upon the sturdy frame and the ruddy cheek as tokens of vulgarity.

The corset is much less obsolete to-day than the rack or the thumbscrew—yet these latter instruments of torture are by far the most humane ; they may maim or kill the victim outright, but are restricted in their effect mainly to one sufferer. While the corset is the vise in which you mold the form of the mother, you thus literally cramp the body and soul of her future offspring.

I have known young girls persistently, month after month, to feed themselves with some vile substance never fit to eat, for the sole purpose of drying up the healthy blood, and making themselves look pale and delicate. If they knew that the bane would mingle in the systems of their future children, blighting their poor little lives with disease and suffering, they would stop aghast. Rather let delicacy of constitution become a brand as disgraceful as that which was stamped upon the brow of the first murderer: he slew his brother in a moment of wrathful envy, but the weakling leaves to her descendants the dark prospect of a few years of suffering and an early death ; which no prudence or wisdom on their part can avert; they are doomed from the beginning by the faults, if not the crimes, of one who should have left them only blessings. When the poor, ignorant Irish girl takes the life of her new-born babe, to conceal her own shame, the stern law punishes her, sometimes, with death— but is the crime a greater one than that of the woman who recklessly destroys her own health, regardless of the rights of those who will become bone of her bone, and flesh of her flesh? Let us elevate the standard of parental morality until people realize how high and noble it is.

CHAPTER TENTH.

"How shall a man escape from his ancestors," says Emerson, "or draw off from his veins the black drop which he drew from his father's or mother's life? It often appears in a family as if all the qualities of the progenitors were potted in several jars, some ruling quality in each son or daughter of the house, and sometimes the unmixed temperament, the rank unmitigated elixir, the family vice is drawn off in a separate individual, and the others are proportionally relieved.— Men are what their mothers made them. You may as well ask a loom which weaves huckaback, why it does not make cashmere, as expect poetry from, this engineer, or a chemical discovery from that jobber. Ask the digger in the ditch to explain Newton's laws: the fine organs of his brain have been pinched by overwork and squalid poverty from father to son for an hundred years. When each comes forth from his mother's womb, the gate of gifts closes behind him. Let him value his hands and feet, he has but one pair. So he has but one future, and that already predetermined in his lobes, and described in that little fatty face, pig-eyed, and squat form. All the privilege and all the legislation of the world cannot meddle or help to make a poet or a prince of him."

Look at the stupidity of the great body of the lower classes; of those who seem never able to direct their own industry, but are always day laborers and servants to others, the hands to the heads; and ask yourself how much of this low grade of faculties has been inherited? We often find like ancestors and like children generation after generation. There are many children of this class who do not rank as imbecile, yet they are never capable of rising above the level in which they were born; and if they were ever brought into mental competition with others, they would rank as simpletons. It is often found that with many idiotic children one or both parents belong to this weak-minded class.

I know an Irish family where the three daughters are so incapable of improvement that they could not learn to become efficient workers at the most common domestic drudgery; with imperturbable good nature, and the best endeavors ceaselessly repeated, they are destined to be bunglers to the end. One of these who lived in the family of a friend, could never be taught to do plain sewing tolerably well; and although she was exceedingly desirous of learning to write, she could not master the accomplishment. She had been taught reading in childhood, yet could not go further than her prayer-book and the children's nursery-tales; all long words she had to spell out or stumble over; yet no one dreams that this girl is idiotic. She ranks every way as respectable as other girls in her station, and her mental defects pass unnoticed. But there is a brother in the family who is an acknowledged imbecile; yet he is only a grade lower in intellect than the sisters.

The mother of these children seems more simple than her daughters; but is a kindly well-disposed old person, liked and befriended by all. Of the father, who is deceased, I could learn nothing except that neither he nor his father could read or write. Should we look to some remarkable cause for the idiocy of the unfortunate son? It is not necessary; he has only inherited a little less sense than his sisters. Weak-mindedness is as much a family trait, as is the slight deafness with which they are nearly all afflicted.

It is said that there are, according to the last census, a less number of idiotic and insane persons amongst the slaves of the South than among any other class in this country. Very possibly this is true. A degree of sense which would answer for the horse, or the dog, would do for the slave; and if he possessed this, he is not likely to be ranked as idiotic. Where a whole class is ranked legally with the brutes, the deficiencies of the individual will easily escape detection; but if he is hopelessly, physically, weak from birth, he is then unlikely to be nurtured into a long life of helplessness.

In the commonwealth of Massachusetts, on the contrary, where there is supposed to be as much of culture, of humanity, and of steady habits, as any where in this country, one in every 321 of the entire population is reported to be either insane, idiotic, deaf and dumb, or blind. When we remember that this does not include the large class who are otherwise defective in body and mind, the statement is truly alarming. Are there, then, so many broken constitutions who have transmitted feeble and defective organizations? Or do they proceed from intemperance in the use of stimulants, narcotics, &c.? Or are we to look for the causes of those deplorable effects from an overtasked mentality of the father; or from untoward circumstances acting on the imagination, and the finely susceptible organism of the mother? Popular prejudice may still ignore the latter cause; but the student of Geoffroy Saint Hilaire will give it due weight and importance.

A large proportion of the idiotic are descended from vicious and degraded progenitors;* but there is a frightful number from the respectable and wealthy classes. In 1856 I was informed by the principal of a school for imbeciles that more than half the children under his charge were the children of bankers—the

---

* In the supplement to a report made to the Massachusetts Senate will be found the following:—

"Out of four hundred and twenty cases of congenital idiocy examined, some information was obtained respecting the condition of the progenitors of three hundred and forty-nine. Now in all these three hundred and forty-nine cases, *save only four*, it was found that one or the other, or both of the progenitors of the unfortunate sufferers had, in some way, widely departed from the conditions of health, and violated the natural laws. That is to say, one or the other, or both of them, were very unhealthy or scrofulous; or they were hereditarily predisposed to affections of the brain, causing temporary insanity; or they had intermarried with blood relations; or they had been intemperate; or had been guilty of sensual excesses, and impaired their constitution. Now it is reasonable to suppose that if more accurate information could have been obtained about the history of the other four cases, some adequate cause would have been found in them also, for the misfortune of the child in the condition of the progenitors."

fathers were bankers themselves, or they held some responsible position in a bank. Three of them came from Philadelphia, and were the offspring of the officers of two banks. "In a large fire insurance company in New York," he continued, "where there are twenty directors, five of their children are idiotic, and some of the richest and most active business men in the city have imbecile children. I could mention a score or more of hopeless idiots whose fathers were either ministers, lawyers, or literary men of note."

"How do you account for such unfortunate results?" I asked.

"I think," he answered, "that the fathers were exhausted, both mentally and physically, not only at the time of conception, but that this had become their customary condition, and that their state acted mesmerically upon the mother, who, with probably an *unwelcome maternity* in prospect, needed consolation, support and sympathy. She found her husband absorbed in banking, lawsuits, theology, letters—her spirits and her health failed, and the child was the victim. But," he continued, "are you aware how large a proportion of the wives of men thus absorbed in business or in a profession are themselves doomed to an early grave? The proportion is very great. The poor young wife is too much alone; her heart needs sympathy, but her husband belongs to the public or to the ledger—so she languishes and dies. Her children suffer probably quite as much through her as from the father. They are weakened by the weakness which is prostrating her."

This statement appeared very startling; but I have

since found it verified. How many men there are, ranking high as statesmen—as men of influential positions and responsible professions, who have buried one, two, three, and even four wives. The proportion is vastly greater among this class than with farmers, mechanics, or day-laborers. Why is this? These men are not blue-beards; they are generally tender and affectionate husbands—at least, when they have time to be such—and their wives are proud of them, and of their reputation. But they always come home fatigued and exhausted; they bring no freshness or buoyancy of spirit to their families. Every day they overtax their mental energies, and every night they come like vampires to feed upon the innocent lives of their unconscious victims. Do the sons of great men seldom become distinguished? How should they, when their fathers thus live upon their vitality from the beginning?

It is orthodox to tell the wife and children to put on the brightest smiles to welcome home their father. He throws himself upon the sofa, weary, jaded and dispirited. The little ones come to caress him, to soothe him, and to give him back their fresh young life. The wife, also, comes and pours into his bosom all the strength which she has been hoarding up for the day. He rises refreshed—a new man; and in this way he recuperates his energies, day after day, and year after year. Is a child sick and fretful?—it must be kept in the nursery. Is the wife feeble and ailing?—she may fade so gradually that he scarcely perceives it. He mourns her death—but the next year there is another fresh young being at his hearthstone, again renewing his strength; so he mounts up as on eagles' wings, but his family are all tending downwards.

Who can doubt the subtle influence of one human being over another? It is apparent in all our social intercourse. No overwrought man can come into a company of healthy, vigorous, cheerful persons, without at once feeling stronger. They may not feel the virtue passing out of them, as Jesus did; nevertheless it does pass from one to the other—*from the positive to the negative.* Nature is always struggling to equalize her forces.

CHAPTER ELEVENTH.

Woman, in Christian countries is no longer regarded as a merely physical being; that is still her rank in the Eastern harem. There she is to be well fed, beautifully dressed, kept plump and fair by a calm and indolent life. Here we have a higher ideal. Her graces must be mental,—spiritualized, etehreal fascination, full of life and charming vivacity. She is no longer a beautiful model of passive flesh and blood; but an ever varying spirit; bewildering you with her changing "moods and tenses."

This popular idea certainly indicates great progress in civilization. But when will woman be regarded as a downright human being, who ought to be educated to bear a reasonable share of human responsibilities, in order to be able to sustain herself with dignity, amid the conflicts, trials and vicissitudes of life?

" Variable as the shade
" By the light quivering aspen made,—
  * * * * * * *
"She sitteth 'ranging golden hair,
" Pleased to find herself so fair."

She should not be held responsible for the absence of higher aspirations, for she is the creation of the spirit of the age. The infant school of life for the girl and the boy are as unlike as the institutions for the instruction of the soldier and the doctor; where the former is taught the art of killing, and the latter the art of healing. These domestic schools are to manufacture two classes of beings,—the pretty, yielding, tractable, inefficient subject, and the robust, self-reliant, domineering, energetic master.

The little girl is shut up in the nursery with her baby-house and her dolls; the only air or exercise she gets is a formal promenade with Bridget and the baby. Occasionally, however, she is dressed in the last Paris costume, and placed in the drawing-room on reception days, to assist in entertaining the company.

"Don't romp, and disarrange it's beautiful dress," says mama, "that's a darling! Come and sit on the sofa and let the ladies see how quiet you can be. No! you cannot run in the garden; you'll tumble your curls, and get as brown as a boy."

Johnny is put astride his father's cane,—with whip in hand, he gallops about in the sunshine and air; red as a rose, active, gay, and graceful as an antelope, he comes cantering into the room to the annoyance of every one, especially of his little sister, whose fine dress suffers from the exuberance of spirits and rough handling.

"What a difference there is between girls and boys!" says the mother, triumphantly. "I am glad Johnny is so much of a boy; but it is a sad trial to my poor nerves."

The energies of the little daughter are all benumbed and repressed. As a child, she is a martyr to clean clothes and a fair complexion; as a young lady, she is sacrificed to tightly-fitting waists and long skirts. At sixteen the physician orders exercise in the open air. She is sent out riding or walking under the especial charge of her brother, who, although he should carry her parasol, and select the best places, cannot save her from damp and draggled garments while walking, nor from a depressing sense of fatigue after riding. Consequently, after a defective early training, she is little benefitted by this boasted exercise; whilst the stout brother, nearly six feet high, feels proud of his strength and manhood, is tenderly patronizing towards the fragile, helpless creature by his side, and talks very feelingly about the God-ordained protection and guidance that man should bestow upon poor, feeble, dependent womanhood!

At eighteen the girl is married; whilst her brother is only a freshman in college. Ten years now, in her nursery,—ten years in his student life. She is a gentle, patient woman; more lovely than ever in her wifely trust and dependence,—more touchingly self-forgetful in her remembrance of the four or five little ones! He is just settled in his profession, a young man of fine promise, all of life before him, manly, self-confident, and sure to win his way to fame and fortune.

Are they equals? Oh, no! She is weak,—he is strong,—she is ignorant, he is wise,—she is dependent, he is independent,—she has no resources within herself, no power of self assertion, no self-reliance, no originality, no inventive genius, no power of generalization or classification, and no heroism except that of passive submission. He has all these qualities, and feels quite competent to make his own circumstances, and to conquer a high position for himself in the battle of life. In short, she is the meek and grateful subject, he, the ruler and law-giver.

Society has been bending these two twigs for nearly thirty years! Do you wonder, then, to see the two full-grown trees so diversely and unalterably inclined?

Give the girl a practical education, a profession, as you do her brother; let her master it before her marriage; teach her to feel, meantime, that maternity is not to be the whole of her life, that she is not physically and mentally fitted for its sacred duties before she is twenty-five or thirty years of age; and that at forty-five she ought to be in the prime of active and efficient mental life. Then she will no longer remain a spiritless being, without aspirations, and without the power of high intellectual attainments.

Make intellectual success in life as honorable for woman as for man, as much demanded by the usages of society, as much a laudable ambition, and it will be found as compatible with her relations as with his.*

---

* "Those who contest against giving women the same education as men, do it on the ground that it would make the women unfeminine, as if Nature had done her work so slightly that it could be so easily unravelled and knit over. In fact, there is a masculine and feminine element in all knowledge, and a man and a woman put to the same study extract only what their nature fits them to see, so that knowledge can be fully orbed only when the two unite in the search and share the spoils." STOWE.

Like man, she will find time for marriage, for the holiest parental duties, for great purposes, and for steady continuous pursuits.

Public opinion, jealous of the interests of husband and child, has decreed that no woman shall persistently follow any profession, or occupation, without losing caste. It has decided that all mental application is incompatible with her home relations, it makes it unwomanly to lead an intellectual life, it trammels her conscience, it appeals to her disinterestedness, it takes into bondage all her highest and most loving traits of heart and head in order to render her cheerfully submissive to what it calls her "woman's destiny."

Public opinion, however, is sometimes very short-sighted. The interests of husband, wife, child, and society are all in harmony. As the mothers are, so will the children be, invalid or robust, imbecile or intellectual, we must make our election, not for the women of the race, but for all that are born of women!*

Hence the injustice of taunting woman, for her enforced mental inferiority must be apparent to the most superficial causist.

"Have you women ever produced a Milton or a Shakespeare?" asks the thoughtless cynic.

"We have not," answers the derided, "but you men have only produced *one* Milton and *one* Shakespeare *more* than we have, in all these ages, and with all your superior advantages! What can you expect of us?"

The only wonder is, that so great a number of wo-

---

* See Appendix C.

men of distinguished abilities should have arisen. We can point even now to names which will rank with the highest in literature, in art, and in science. But women are only just beginning to feel that they may become successful competitors of men; and men are slowly learning to think this may be inevitable, and not objectionable.

Let this generation pass away, and there are many of its daughters who will have written their names high in the book of achievement!

"Stand on the sea-shore," says Emerson, "and observe the rising tide; one white-crested billow rolls in after another, each advancing beyond its predecessor; presently one mountain wave overtops all the rest, and leaves its marks high up on the beach :—look a little longer, behold, the whole ocean has risen to the same level!"

So it is with the tides of human progress. The advancing waves in literature were the Martineaus, the Brownings, the Brontes, and the Beechers; in art, the Hosmers, and the Bonheurs; in science, the Somervilles and the Mitchels; then came the great mountain wave of humanity, Florence Nightingale,—and the whole troubled sea of womanhood is eagerly pressing up towards their level!

CHAPTER TWELFTH.

"There must be a book for women, written by a woman," says Michelet. We are made sensible of the truth of this remark, by reading his works on "Love," and on "Woman." These pictures of home affections, and their various relations, are often full of poetry, pathos, and charming sentiment. The two books are one; they are a series of simple touching idyls of the household.

We give all honor to the man, who, in the heart of France, with its lost faith in the sacredness of the marriage institution, has tried to write purely and beautifully of love and womanhood!

M. Michelet finds society overwhelmed by its marriages of convenience on the one hand, and on the other, crushed to a deeper degradation by a repudiation of marriage altogether. Under these circumstances he invites the man,—the savan of thirty, satiated with the world, to seek a new happiness in wedlock. He is to find an innocent child of sixteen, to transplant her to a rural paradise, shut her away from all other influences, and by devoted love on his part, to make her satisfied to live absorbed in himself. She is to adopt his views, to be moulded, transformed and ennobled by his influence.

This is his ideal marriage. It is charming, certainly; but what is it? It is only a good deal higher, and a little more desirable than the old one; but it has no basis of permanency. The author himself feels this, and expects all the various casualties which are almost certain to occur.

The woman never rises to a condition of self-reliance, never to a dignified self-respect, or to any worthy individuality. How could she? She has not been educated for this! Her husband never truly esteems her, trusts her, or regards her in any sense as an equal. He merely attempts to adore her; to reverence and deify her; but with rather doubtful success.

Is this the highest thought on marriage, that closest and most durable of earthly ties? It may do for effete and artificial France,—possibly for a large portion of Southern Europe; but any community educated ever so slightly to the idea of self-government, to personal activity, and responsibility, must repudiate this union, as shallow, though portrayed with all the fascination of the most popular French philosopher.

First, woman is not created an invalid. M. Michelet is a profound student of nature and of French life; but his first predicate, that woman is, by the peculiarity of her constitution an invalid, is a serious error; for it arraigns the justice and goodness of a wise and beneficent Creator. Health must be the normal condition of the whole race. Wherever there is physical suffering, it has been caused by the transgression of the physical laws. So if women suffer more than men, it must be that they have sinned more against the conditions of health. Let us bring the sturdiest young forest trees into our houses, and plant them in the artificial heat and the unnatural shade which we procure for our wives and daughters, and we shall see them too wither, grow up slenderly and become beautifully fragile. It is easy to become an invalid, if one will but take the right means; even M. Michelet is aware of this, for he speaks of some women " who have made men of themselves" and are healthy. His servant girl from the country, fresh and strong, is, on the whole, a much better type of womanhood than her mistress. True, she is rude and uneducated, but the lady is as uneducated, more characterless, and with a namby-pamby helplessness in addition.

It is time we repudiated the idea that feebleness and refinement are inseparable. Good health is quite compatible with the highest mental culture, and with all the graces of cultivated manners.

It requires very little heroism in a woman to bear with patience the pains and disabilities imposed on her by Nature; for they only affect her physical system; whereas those imposed by man often pertain to her affections—to her mental rights, and cause more acute anguish than any bodily suffering could produce.

Let Nature limit us by such disabilities as she will; but let not man fetter us by his clumsy iron manacles of law and custom. Give the same freedom socially, and intellectually, to women which men enjoy,—teach them to use it for the best development of all their powers,—give them scope for action, purposes and aims worthy to enlist their highest aspirations, and we shall hear much less of feeble health. God never made a constitutional invalid! Certainly, not a great class of weak, helpless, pre-ordained sick people.

Secondly. There can be no true marriage except between those who are essentially equals. A child-wife is a pretty plaything. She cannot be a fitting companion for head or heart.

There may be something attractive in the thought of moulding another being to meet your own ideal. All young persons are plastic and impressible; and whether it be wife, child, or any other loved one, it is delightful to watch its progress. But M. Michelet's wife and child are one; there is the same pleasure in forming the character of each; but neither of them are expected to outgrow a dependent nature. She is expected to be "timid, docile, and obedient" to the end; a loving, receptive nature, with no vigor or originality. You are never to destroy "the velvet down of the soul" by imparting too much knowledge.

It is all very well in educating youth of either sex, to have regard to their tender years, and to choose for them appropriate subjects of thought. But all truth which is good for man is good also for woman—that which can ennoble the one must ennoble the other. Doubtless they are not alike—not identical in mental traits; but if they are not equals in the vigor and strength of mental life and activity, then the truest and highest marriage is impossible. A union devoid of the highest friendship must also be devoid of that most ennobling passion—love. The great soul itself must love greatness, and seek it in all its intimate and dear companionship. Unless the world can change its ideal of womanly capabilities, it can have but few exalted marriages—but few children worthily born.

What a deplorable picture is drawn by our author in his second book, of the inferiority of woman. "Soon, if we do not take care," he says, "in spite of casual meetings, there will be no longer two sexes, but two peoples." Has he found a cure for this? A man may love his child or his child-wife for her pretty little artless ways; but will he love her for those things when she is old and wrinkled?

If you would draw the man of the world into a truly worthy and permanent union, it must be with his peer. If you would elevate woman to this rank, it must be by giving her a purpose, motives, activities, self-reliance and individuality. Then the bond may last so long as memory and consciousness remain. Then the woman will find something to do after her children are grown—when she is no longer young;— then she will become the life of his soul, and together they will create new thoughts, new deeds; then, if like the model wives of history, she cannot bear him on her shoulders from impending destruction, she might assist him to bear manfully any reverse of fortune; might convince him how infinitely more important to a business man is a character for integrity and honor than a large capital without it; might aid him to withstand the pernicious example of successful but fraudulent gain; of corrupt morals in high places; might help him to train up their children's children, thus promoting individual happiness and human progress; might make this period of life an intellectual harvest to herself as to her husband.

CHAPTER THIRTEENTH.

M. MICHELET has stripped the very fig-leaf from poor humanity; exposing to view the strong passions and the weak will of man, without any beneficial end; unlike the skilful surgeon, who probes and cuts in order to cure, he merely states the facts, leaving the penalties resulting from an abuse of his nature. unexplained.

The following paragraph contains more real and useful information for those who need it, than the whole volume just referred to.

"There is a marked antagonism of the nervous and generative systems. Intense mental application, involving great waste of the nervous tissues, and a corresponding consumption of nervous material for their repair, is accompanied by a cessation of the productive principle. And also that *undue production involves cerebral inactivity*. The first result of a morbid excess in this direction is a headache, which may be taken to indicate that the brain is out of repair; this is followed by stupidity; should the disorder continue, imbecility supervenes, ending occasionally in insanity and death."*

* " New Theory of Population."

Here, also, is a gem from Carlyle, wonderfully suggestive; we would recommend it to the attention of those who consider sensuous pleasures the most desirable good of life.

"How true is that old fable of the Sphinx, who sat by the wayside, propounding her riddle to the passers by, which, if they could not answer, she destroyed them. Such a Sphinx in this life of ours, to all men and societies of men. Nature, like the Sphinx, is of womanly celestial loveliness and tenderness; the face and bosom of a goddess, but ending in claws and the body of a lioness. There is in her a celestial beauty; which means celestial order, pliancy to wisdom; but there is also a darkness and ferocity which are infernal. She is a goddess, but one not yet disimprisoned; one still half imprisoned,—the inarticulate, lovely still incased in the inarticulate chaotic. How true! And does she not propound her riddles to us? Of each man she asks daily, in mild voice, yet with terrible significance: "Knowest thou the meaning of this Day? What thou canst do to-day; wisely attempt to do?" Nature, Universe, Destiny, Existence, however we name this grand unnamable fact, in the midst of which we live and struggle, is as a heavenly bride and conquest to the wise and brave, to them who can discern her behests and do them; a destroying fiend to them who cannot. Answer her riddle, it is well with thee. Answer it not, pass on regarding it not, it will answer itself; the solution for thee is a thing of teeth and claws; Nature is a dumb lioness, deaf to thy pleadings, fiercely devouring. Thou art not now her victorious bridegroom; thou art her mangled victim, scattered on the precipices, as a slave found treacherous, recreant ought to be, and must."

The authoress does not feel called upon to become a moral martyr in this cause; therefore will only indicate a few of the questions which might be put by the Inexorable.

To the man of sixty-five or seventy, who marries a young girl, she might say, " Knowest thou not the penalty of thus outraging one of Nature's most holy laws ? Study it out, make reparation by a life of purity and continency, or thy days in this world are numbered."

To him who allows reason and conscience to become subservient to the animal propensities, she might say, " Forbear ! or paralysis may strike thee down in the prime of thy life."

Again, " Art thou a man well reputed, endorsed and accredited by good society, yet conscious of blight and mildew feeding at thy heart?—decide, then, how many tons of popular adulation will weigh in the balance against one grain of self-respect."*

" Miserable father," says the Sphinx, " dost thou recognize thy own vices exaggerated in thy children ?— dost thou see the seeds of hateful passions budding and blosssoming even in their infant lives?—dost thou stand shocked and appalled by fearful presentiments of their disgraceful future ? Solve this riddle, then—

---

* Is there any paradox in this ? A man buoyed up like a feather on the breath of fashion, at the same time drawn down like a drowning man under the dark waters of remorse by the mill-stone of secret shame.

which is the most potent, the taint of hereditary vice, or the disinfectant of an unresting conscientious education?"

Ah! the Inexorable will have all her questions answered; or she will sit forever by the wayside of life propounding them and torturing us with her mysteries, and making the solution of them to us, indeed, "a thing of teeth and claws!"

There is another beautiful Eastern fable of Adam and Eve when they were first expelled from Paradise. Desolate and homeless, they wandered amid the burning sands of the desert, till exhausted they sank down under the unimpeded rays of the scorching sun, and, hand in hand, they slept. Michael, the archangel, was passing that way; his heart was moved to pity; he would help them all he could. He was bearing seeds at the time, to be planted in various parts of the earth; so he scattered many kinds of them around about where the helpless sleepers lay, and passed quickly on.

By-and-bye, as Satan was passing to and fro in the earth, he came also, and looked on the sleepers. "Ah!" said he, "Adam and Eve I know, and these sands I know; but what are these?" He bent over and carefully scanned the seeds. "At any rate, it will be safe to cover them up," mused the Father of Evil. So, with his cloven foot he scooped up the sand, and buried every little seed; thus they were nicely planted. Straightway after he had departed, they sprang up rapidly into shrubs and trees. Some of them burst forth into flower, and all of them were covered with thick foliage, so that when the sleepers awoke, they found themselves in the midst of a beautiful oasis in the desert.

Thus the master spirit of evil in the world, Ignoranc, seems to have been always endeavoring to cover up the results of human experience. This hydra-headed monster tries to bury causes, and to have them forgotten as things that have passed away; but when effects spring from them as their direct fruits, he whispers, " these came from the dark earth, where everything is mysterious, we know not whence they arose." So mankind were deluded, and looked on stupidly, and almost ceased to believe in the inseparable bond of cause and effect.

This covering up process, however, has everywhere planted the seeds of both good and evil; they have taken deep root in the rich soil of the human heart, and after these many ages they have sprung up, not simply, an oasis in the desert, but a vast extent of country, covered with every variety of growth, so luxuriant, rank, and quick to decay, that a moral miasma is imminent! The question is thus forced home with startling emphasis, how can we best clear away the noisome and useless plants,—the low, creeping, tangled undergrowth, which destroys beauty, and impedes progress.

If causes had not been persistently buried out of sight, like the roots of vegetation, the result must have been less magnificent than at present. Now the problems of human life are all on a grand complicated scale,—then they would have been direct, simple and narrow. We have been gaining every way in the hight, depth, and breadth of experiences; and the grandest intellect may bend all its energies to the solution of the intricate social and moral questions of the day. Thus is the overruling hand of a wise providence forever controlling the affairs of mankind. Despite the vices and the sufferings of even the lowest and most thoughtless classes, their destiny is still tending upward.

The magnificent discoveries in all other sciences, must quicken thought in the direction of the greatest and most practical of them all,—that of human development. Since the good angels are still every where scattering their celestial seeds,—since the beneficent Ruler of all, is still sending His fruitful sunshine and his quickening showers; we need not despond! There is also a sublime and cheering movement, in the intelligent and active co-operation, of the combined intentness of many humane minds working together heroically to further human progress.

CHAPTER FOURTEENTH.

An article appeared several years since in the "Westminster Review" entitled "A New Theory of Population;"* in which the author undertakes to show how the perfect and complete graduation of the number of inhabitants, to the best development and the highest happiness of all, is to be continually secured.

"When from lowness of organization," says this writer, "the ability to contend with danger is small there must be great fertility, to compensate for the consequent mortality; otherwise the race would die out. When on the contrary, high endowments give much capacity for self-preservation there needs a corresponding low degree of fertility." Thus he assumes that the forces which tend to multiply the race, and the forces destructive to individual life, are antagonistic,—and vary inversely. He confirms his hypothesis by facts and illustrations from the vegetable, and the animal kingdoms.

This article embodies a vast amount of observation, learning, and research, in every department of natural

* Herbert Spencer.

history; and abounds with close and logical arguments deduced from the wide range of knowledge thus obtained. The conclusion arrived at, is very encouraging; we cannot render a greater service to our reader, than to give the summing up entire.*

Natural and physical causes are all potent and can never be set aside. We would give them everywhere their due weight and influence; but man is by nature an intelligent and voluntary actor,—of course within the range of the established laws. If he would secure his own highest good, he must do it intelligently, and voluntarily by conforming to the physical and moral principles which alone can establish this good.

The wisdom of Providence, by which all things are made self-adjusting, must finally bring the race into the conditions which will secure its constant progressive development. But if the individual ever attains any superior good for himself, it must be through his own earnest effort. If he would reach anything grander than the present, he must understand both the end and the means, and then work towards the desired result.

Every great man must work out his own greatness. Nature plants the seeds within him, but he must nourish and foster them, as the gardener does his finest trees, or there will be neither choice fruit nor rare growth.

Nature can do many things well, but science and art co-operating with her, upon the basis of her own laws, can outstrip her in the race, and carry the work

---

* See Appendix E.

infinitely higher than she, unaided, could do. She produces the crab apple, which they improve into the pippin, and all the other delicious varieties.

I would, therefore, urge the thought of individual responsibility everywhere; and especially in the parental relation. In some far off golden age, Nature may regulate the number of children which shall be desirable in each household: at present, every family must decide that matter for itself. Parents may tamper with the life, or the reason, of an unborn child; but it is immeasurably better to learn that self-control which will give them only the number of offspring, that can be religiously welcomed, and trained with the care indispensible to their true well-being.

Nature, unassisted, in the course of centuries, may so arrange the affairs of mankind as to secure the utmost harmony; but each generation, if it will, can do this for itself. Each human pair should decide how many children are desirable, how many, under all the family circumstances, will contribute to the best good of the whole. The age, the health, the occupation of either or both of the parents, and the pecuniary matters, are all modifying conditions which should limit the number of offspring.

Children, *per se*, are undoubtedly blessings. The more numerous and close our social ties the better; and he who has nobly disciplined his own nature may reasonably expect worthy descendants. Life in itself is a good, and the new being should feel grateful that it has been conferred upon him. The parent, also, lives again in his child, sharing all his interests with the keenest zest. Thus the invisible bond of relationship widens and deepens the experiences of each; it creates a growth which makes room for the more impersonal relationships and friendships with the great human family.

"I rejoice in your marriage," said a great man to a young friend, "not that it will make your life more happy, but that it will widen the compass of your experiences, and give you a larger and a more natural growth."

Yes, children are blessings; real and genuine to the worthy. Every magnanimous heart feels repaid for the care bestowed upon them; even the anxieties which must follow all young people, placed as ours are, in the great garden, where there are fruits of both good and evil, will confirm this decision,—grief, anguish, and disappointment cannot revoke it; for in all these are recognized life's wholesome discipline to us and to them.

Admitting all this, there may be many reasons why a large family is not always desirable. The mother's health may be in peril; too frequent maternity may make it almost certain that she will sink at last, leaving her young family without the fostering care of a mother's love. There may be, also, hereditary weaknesses, which it would be unwise to entail on others.

The consumptive husband may leave his wife with a family, in whom the seeds of death are surely planted, to struggle on hopeless and alone, until the grave closes over every object of earthly affection, and she is left desolate.

Again, a poor laborer with no hope or expectation beyond poverty, will bequeath to the world his dozen children, who grow up untaught, undisciplined, because neither parent had time, means, or ability to bestow upon them; and thus society is every where injured by the acts of the weak, the vicious, and the improvident.

Every reflecting man should be able to control his passions by his reason. It is this which constitutes his superiority over the brute creation. It is not enough that he is able to see the right and desirable course, he must be able to walk therein, putting aside all counter impulses, like a superior being, or he becomes more ignoble than the unreasoning animals, who know no higher law, therefore, break none. There is no dignity in man's rational nature if he cannot rule himself by its dictates.

These ideas may be scouted by the self-indulgent, ridiculed by the thoughtless, and ignored by the fastidious; they may, even, meet with grave rebuke by the conscientious, but timidly conservative. Yet they are the thoughts of the age on this subject. Noble and far-seeing minds recognize them;* the unselfish and the magnanimous already accept them as the practical rule of life; they have sprung into existence from a thousand different sources, and, like leaven, they are destined to pervade and to elevate society.

It is the right, the duty of every man to decide for himself, as an intelligent and responsible moral agent, whether he can conscientiously accept the relation of parent,—more especially it is the right of every wife to do this. The perils and the cares are largely

* See Appendix F.

hers; her rights and her duties are commensurate with these. Will she become the mother of one, two, three, or half a score of children? It is her solemn privilege to decide this matter as the equal, the peer, of her husband—with no more rights than he, certainly with no less. The social relations of the two must require the concurrence of both, in all matters of moment, and neither has the right of coercion. Humanity has been cursed long enough by its poor tear-washed children; while they still come to us as the heavy penalties of unrestrained impulses, whether in wedlock or out of it. God help them and the race.

How low have we fallen, then, when theory rises no higher than practice,—when our teachers give us no better instruction than the every day practice of the ignorant? Nay, the poor wife is taught that in feebleness, as in health, her husband's will must be her law, that she must accept maternity always as the one condition of her wifely estate. The time will come when this code of wedded morality will be abhorred; people will think higher, will acknowledge a self-sovereignty as omnipotent over the flesh, as it is now thought, it should be over the spirit,—for there is a steady growth upwards, and a worthy idea which has once gained the ear of the people, must make its way into their hearts.*

While we are dwelling upon the causes of inherited weaknesses, it would be fatal to overlook that which lies at the foundation of all others. Think, then, of each successive child, dating its life from no high-

---

* See Appendix G.

er impulse than sensuality, the main-spring of its being, tempered at such an altar, can it be expected to possess that most difficult, most God-like attribute, self control? Yet these are only some of the streams flowing from that great turbid fountain of inheritance, a fountain so dark and deep that we have scarcely dared attempt to fathom it; but the stream can never run clear until the source be purified.

The remedy is safe and practicable. Give to the youth a high aim in life, and he will cease to be profligate. There is as much in the principle of counter-irritants in morals, as in medicine. Employ the mind in other directions; give it change, rest, stimulus in some worthy cause, hold the body in check by plain food and the pure element, by fresh air, much bathing, and abundant exercise. A strong sense of right, and an earnest purpose to pursue it, added to such discipline, would be omnipotent.

A well-devised system of gymnastics would, also, have a most valuable influence in the development and invigoration of the frame during the approach to adolescence; and would be capable of correcting, or, at least, keeping in check many unfavorable tendencies. Such a system would be well worthy of the attention of those who are engaged in the education of youth.

CHAPTER FIFTEENTH.

PROBABLY the present extravagant and luxurious mode of living involves so great an outlay of means that men with families are obliged often to sacrifice health and strength in order to meet it. Yet this a condition of things of their own creating. A perverted love of the beautiful, and a passion for elegant and expensive surroundings, appear to have become a national trait in the upper classes of this country. American women have acquired a reputation all over Europe, for extravagant habits and a lavish expenditure for personal adornments. This unenviable reputation must react upon themselves; many of their daughters will be obliged to remain unmarried; for, with the prospect before them of an extravagant wife and an expensive family, bachelors will not have the courage to "propose." Nature is, however, always true to herself. The beautiful, talented and vivacious girl requires no external adornments; her native loveliness will always attract an admiring circle, while her dull, uninteresting and overdressed companion is neglected.

As mind is superior to matter, so are mental accomplishments and personal beauty superior to—-

"Robes of satin and Brussels lace,
Rubies, diamonds, or pretty face."

This view of the subject might very properly rank under the head of domestic economy; and the question be asked, if parents were able to bestow upon their daughters sound constitutions, personal graces, and good mental abilities, would not such qualities conduce more to their true and permanent happiness than great wealth without them ?*

If the choice were submitted to the daughters, we apprehend there would be but little doubt as to which way they would decide. The heart of woman yearns for love as its natural aliment. Her keen appreciation of this noble sentiment enables her to detect at

---

* "Mamas anxious to make their daughters attractive, could scarcely choose a course more fatal than that which sacrifices the body to the mind. Either they disregard the tastes of the opposite sex, or else their conception of those tastes is erroneous. Men care comparatively little for erudition in women; but very much for physical beauty, and good nature and sound sense. How many conquests does the bluestocking make through her extensive knowledge of history ? .... But rosy cheeks and laughing eyes are great attractions. The liveliness and good humor that overflowing health produces, go a great way towards establishing attachments. Every one knows of cases where bodily perfections, in the absence of all other recommendations, have incited a passion that carried all before it; but scarcely any one can point to a case where mere intellectual acquirements, apart from moral or physical attributes, have secured such a feeling. The truth is, that out of many elements uniting in various proportions to produce in a man's breast that complex emotion which we call love, the strongest are those produced by physical attractions; the next in order of strength are those produced by moral attractions; the weakest are those produced by intellectual attractions; and even these are dependent much less upon acquired knowledge than on natural faculty—quickness, wit, insight."—Education: Physical, Moral and Intellectual. By Herbert Spencer. Page 279.

once the real from the spurious; and it is only under the influence of the former, she well knows, that men are constrained to surrender themselves unconditionally at the shrine of wit and beauty.

A gentleman who possessed a fine person, polished manners, and a large fortune, was asked by a lady whose children he was admiring, why he did not marry.

"Madam," he replied, "I should be most happy to do so, if I could find a young lady, who with an agreeable person combined refined and cultivated tastes, and high-minded, honorable principles."

Beautiful attributes, certainly; but not so rare in good society, as many bachelors endeavor to persuade themselves, in order to hide their own selfishness. But to enable one to recognize high moral, or intellectual qualities in another, it is necessary to possess them, in some degree, one's self.

Let us look into the conduct and habits of this class of single gentlemen about town, and endeavor to ascertain on what they found their claims to high-minded and honorable wives; also, what is their standard of honorable conduct.

Do they consider it honorable, to bestow all their politeness and attentions on young married ladies; making themselves perfect bankrupts, with not even a rag of civility to throw to the single ones? Is it honorable to flirt with a fiancée, for the mere pleasure of gratifying one's vanity, and making her lover jealous? Is it honorable to abuse the confidence of a friend, by trying to corrupt the principles of his wife, by forcing costly presents on her acceptance? Is it honorable to gain the affections of an innocent young girl, and after an engagement of many years, to desert her, in order to marry the daughter of a wealthy man; knowing that the antecedents of the parents are not creditable; or that a tendency to insanity or disease runs in the family?

These questions, it will be perceived, are confined to social relations. Many others might be asked in relation to the standard of honor which obtains in fashionable Club-Houses, where these aspirants for high-minded and honorable wives " most do congregate."

Every community has its own social customs, which are quite as positive and distinct as its local opinions and prejudices; unconsciously adopted at first, they are in the end tenaciously defended, and whoever dares to attack them is regarded as a maligner. The rural districts have their own peculiar vices, doubtless, but large towns certainly have theirs. One custom which prevails extensively in cities, is most pernicious and evil in its influences. I refer to the constant and intimate attentions of unmarried gentlemen to married ladies. Society tolerates this gallantry,— even fosters, protects and defends it, as a refined stimulus to social life. The husband is pleased with the attentions which his wife commands; the wife is vain of her power, and of her conquests; while her rivals may envy or admire the piquancy of her Platonic friendships. If she is gay and attractive, a whole bevy of single gentlemen become her constant attendants; they make her morning calls; ride with her; walk with her; attend her to the ball; to the opera; or meet her there; always smiling and elegant, as her very welcome satellites. The husband smiles, too, dreaming only of his own ease and freedom, and of his wife's popularity. Thus we have created and tolerated that order of "nice young men" who become attached to other men's wives, but for themselves, despise matrimony.

The sharp tongue of the country-town would soon talk such men out of its borders. Such neighborly supervision may have its inconveniences; but in a community where everybody knows just what families, or members of families attend church,—just which ladies have four new bonnets a year, and which contrive to get along with two or three,—this class of the genus homo, at least has no chance of an existence. Every whisper of scandal awakens an echo of warning in each household; but when a city has merged the individuality of its hundreds of thousands, it has no protection for the thoughtless young wife, whose husband, absorbed in his own pursuits, leaves her to stem the current of ruinous social precedents as best she can. Now and then we are startled and shocked by some domestic tragedy; but it is like a pebble thrown into a great stream,—it is covered up in a moment, and we are again watching the dancing bubbles that float and sparkle on its surface.

Young married ladies may feel flattered by the attentions of fashionable single gentlemen,—may delight in rivaling the fairest maidens as belles and coquettes; but if they knew the utter unscrupulousness of some of this class, they would sooner trust themselves to the influence of the poison-exhaling Upas, or to the death-dealing blast of the scorching Simoon, than to court, or receive their attentions. "It has been suggested," says Margaret Fuller, "by men who were pained by seeing bad men admitted freely to the society of modest women, thereby encouraged to vice by impunity, and corrupting the atmospheres of homes,—that there should be a Senate of matrons in each city and town, who should decide what candidates were fit for admission to their houses and the society of their daughters.

"Such a plan might have excellent results, but it argues a moral dignity and decision, which does not yet exist, and needs to be induced by knowledge and reflection. It has been the tone to keep women ignorant on these subjects, or when they were not, to command that they should seem so. 'It is indelicate,' says the father or husband, 'to inquire into the private character of such an one. It is sufficient that I do not think him unfit to visit you.' And so he introduces there a man whose shame is written on his brow, as well as the open secret of the whole town; and presently, if *respectable* still, and rich enough, gives him his daughter to wife. The mother affects ignorance, 'supposing he is no worse than most men.' The daughter *is* ignorant; something in the mind of the new spouse seems strange to her, but she supposes it is 'woman's lot' not to be perfectly happy in her affections; she has always heard, 'men could not understand women,' so she weeps alone, or takes to dress, or the duties of the house. The husband of course makes no avowal, and dreams of no redemption.

"Let every woman who has once begun to think on

this subject, examine herself—see whether she does not suppose virtue possible and necessary to man, and whether she would not desire for her son a virtue that aimed at a fitness for a divine life, and involved, if not asceticism, that degree of power over the lower self, which shall 'not exterminate the passions, but keep them chained at the feet of reason.' The passions, like fire, are a bad master; but confine them to the hearth and the altar, and they give life to the social economy, and make each sacrifice meet for heaven.

"When many women have thought upon this subject, some will be fit for the Senate—and one such Senate in operation would affect the morals of the civilized world.

"At present I look to the young. As preparatory to the Senate, I should like to see a society of novices, such as the world has never yet seen, bound by no oath, wearing no badge. In place of an oath they should have a religious faith in the capacity of men for virtue; instead of a badge, should wear in the heart a firm resolve not to stop short of the destiny promised him as a son of God. Their service should be action and conservatism, not of old habits, but of a better nature, enlightened by hopes that daily grow brighter.

"If sin was to remain in the world, it should not be by their connivance at its stay, or one moment's concession to its claims.

"They should succor the oppressed, and pay to the upright the reverence due in hero-worship by seeking to emulate them. They would not denounce the willingly bad, but they would not be with them, for the two classes could not breathe the same atmosphere.— They would heed no detention from the time-serving, the worldly; and the timid; and they would love no pleasures that were not innocent and capable of good fruit."

CHAPTER SIXTEENTH.

If a few men are vampires, feeding on the nervous energy of their families, many women are worse than millstones about the necks of their husbands. Every woman who enters married life with no other purpose in view than social enjoyment and personal adornment—who spends her days alternating between lassitude and company as frivolous as herself, is a heavy drag upon her husband. If he is ambitious and energetic, and aspires to anything higher, his soul must revolt at such a helpmeet.

We know that it is poetical to designate woman as a parasite—a clinging tendril, seeking support from the sturdy strength of manhood. Yet retributive Nature has decreed that the parasite shall feed mainly on decayed life; and that wherever it flourishes, it superinduces disease and death. Many a noble oak or elm has been sapped of its strength by the beautiful vine which crept lovingly about it, challenging its protection and support.

In some of the forests of South America may be seen high columns of vegetation in the form of cylinders. This phenomena is produced by the decay of a large forest tree, which had been enveloped by parasites. Poor creeping things, they not only hung upon its limbs a dead-weight, but they absorbed its vitality. Fit emblem of man's fate, when he takes to himself a wife, weak, indolent and selfish. In vain he immolates himself a willing martyr on the altar of matrimony, if there be no sympathetic heart or co-worker to share its responsibilities and its duties. His vain, frivolous wife spends her mornings shopping or making calls, (leaving her children to the coarse influence of hirelings, where their health or their morals may be corrupted,) and her afternoons indolently reclining on a sofa, reading the weakest of weekly magazines. If he has a taste for reading, and would like to keep up with the current literature of the day, or the progress of the age, and lead her on to congenial pursuits, he has no opportunity; for one night she must be accompanied to a party, another to a concert or opera, and the next she has calls at home: so the season passes with little leisure and no improvement, but with a slow and ceaseless wear upon the strong man's mind and body. Her weakness is as fatal to him as the "shirt of Nessus"!

An energetic business occupation strengthens man or woman. Over-care and over-exertion are evils—but indolence is an evil tenfold more destructive. Few women would ever become so absorbed in any business, that some months of comparative leisure at home would not seem like a pleasant rest and change. There would be a positive benefit in the transition, which need be only a partial one, while the mother nourished the unborn hope like a holy thing in her bosom, ready to do, and to bear unselfishly for the sake of one dearer than self. Ah, there is no true incompatibility between an honorable life-calling, properly conducted, and the most faithful and conscientious discharge of every maternal obligation. The devotee of fashion will be much more likely to neglect her children than the earnest woman who finds too much value in life to be willing to idle it away.— Business now is the Moloch to which men sacrifice their lives. They must do this to maintain their families in the position they desire ; but when and women are co-workers in business and in the home, there need be no immolations on the mammon altar for the benefit of the family—they all may harmonize and prosper together. Neither the husbands worn out with over-work, nor the wives devoured by listlessness. Then also may come children who will not only love but *respect* their parents, and bring new honors to the family name.

CHAPTER SEVENTEENTH.

In a little company of savans, one evening, the conversation turned upon the causes of various social evils. One gentleman designated the immorality which frequently exists in the marriage relation, as a most prolific source of more open vice. His strong statement was received with incredulity. He turned to a physician of eminent standing, and asked, "Doctor, how many children of the whole number born in this city, do you believe have been cordially welcomed by both parents?"

"Not one in ten."

"How many mothers of large families, have probably been desirous of many children?"

"Perhaps one in fifty;" answered the Doctor.

"About what would be the proportion of births, as compared with the present, if the whole matter were left to the choice of the wives?"

"Hah!" said the Doctor, drawing a hard breath through his teeth, and starting to his feet, "not a sixth part."

Two other physicians present considered this a pretty correct estimate; and the small band of wise men were divided in opinion, as to whether it would be safe to give women a decisive voice in this matter. There were a few who contended that, in that event, the world would become depopulated.

Yet there are very few women without enough of the maternal instinct, to make them regard some children as an exceeding blessing; and no happily married wife would long be content with a childless home. The perils, sufferings, and anxieties, incident to the condition, are counted as nothing, when weighed in the balance, against such an evil.

Yet the young girl is scarcely ever ready for these new responsibilities, during the first few years of her marriage. The trials and cares connected with the little one, prove so exhausting, that she is in no haste to repeat them; and when one after another, has been unwillingly added to the number, there is but little chance of her ever becoming the mother of a child truly desired. After months of weeping, peevishness, and low spirits—there may be joy at last, " that a man is born into the world;" but the son is not likely to give his mother much joy, after having been nurtured all his ante-natal life, on such bitter thoughts. As well might we expect the blossom that had been blasted by the north wind, to bring forth good fruit.

It may frequently be observed in some families, that after an interval of several years, there has come at last a truly welcome child; one who proves to be infinitely superior to all which preceeded it.

A young married couple in the State of Ohio, had two little girls, pleasant and bright children enough, but neither beautiful nor any way remarkable. The attention of the parents, meantime, had been directed to the subject of parental responsibilities; they were thoughtful, earnest, conscientious persons, who received every new theory with avidity, that they could make practical and self-improving. Accordingly, they resolved to have no more children, until they could hope to confer on them a superior nature.

In the zeal of their earnestness, they announced this determination to confidential friends; they also ventured prophecies respecting the improved character of the expected child. Nor were they disappointed. The little girl answered all their anticipations, was beautiful, sprightly, and precocious; she bids fair to out-strip both her sisters in intellectual attainments. True there had been, meantime, years of growth and maturity to the parents; this, in itself, must have benefited the child; but who will doubt that their harmonious and joyful hope, contributed much also?

In sacred writ we find this idea illustrated. "Let it be unto thine handmaiden even as thou sayest," answered Mary the mother of Jesus at the Annunciation. Hannah, the mother of Samuel, is another case in point. Some of the most holy men of modern history, missionaries and martyrs, were, like Samuel, "asked of the Lord," and dedicated to His service even before birth, by mothers whose hearts were fired with a holy zeal for the cause of Christ and for the redemption of mankind.

Allow to wives more independence of character, more individuality—give them time and opportunities for self-culture—teach them that on themselves depend the future happiness or misery of their offspring—give them also a womanly right in their children, and we shall find the maternal instinct both strong and sacred. Children will then become more beautiful, more healthy, and harmonious in body and in mind. While the mothers are only passive subjects, the children must have craven souls; the child of the serf will ever cleave to the soil from inevitable necessity. Nature's retribution is thus written on successive generations; for it was ordained from the beginning, that plant, and animal, and man, should bring forth seed, "each after his kind." The weak and inefficient woman must therefore bear children as inertly passive in nature as herself.

"Man," says Margaret Fuller, "in the order of time, was developed first; as energy comes before harmony, power before beauty. Woman was therefore under his care as an elder. He might have been her guardian and teacher.

"But as human nature goes not straightforward, he misunderstood and abused his advantages, and became her temporal master instead of her spiritual sire.

"On himself came the punishment. He educated woman more as a servant than as a daughter, and found himself a king without a queen.

"The children of this unequal union showed unequal natures, and more and more men seemed sons of the handmaid rather than of princes.*

---

* This view of the subject might account for the abject dispositions of the offspring of white fathers and slave mothers. It has been frequently stated, as a proof of the inferiority of this mixed race, that no

"At last there were so many Ishmaelites that the rest grew frightened and indignant. They laid the blame on Hagar, and drove her into the wilderness. But yet there were none the less Ishmaelites for that.

"At last men became a little wiser, and saw that the infant Moses was in every case saved by the pure instincts of a mother's breast. For as too much adversity is better for the moral nature than too much prosperity, woman, in this respect, dwindled less than man, though, in other respects, still a child in leading strings.

"So man did her more and more justice, and grew more and more kind.

"But yet, his habits and his will corrupted by the past, he did not clearly see that woman was half himself, that her interests were identical with his, and that by the law of their common being, he could never reach his true proportions while she remained in any wise shorn of hers.

"And so it has gone on to our day, both ideas developing, but more slowly than they would under a clearer recognition of truth and justice, which would have permitted the sex their due influence on one another, and mutual improvement from more dignified relations.

---

able or heroic men, have ever sprung up among them. Now it is a well known law of Nature, that the moral characteristics of the mother, are generally transmitted to the son; and those of the father. to the daughter; therefore. it may be presumed that the white father transmits a very low degree of moral nature to his quadroon daughter. Hence, it follows that the latter cannot transmit to her son, that which she does not possess herself.

" Wherever there was pure love, the natural influences were, for a time, restored.

" Wherever the poet or the artist gave free scope to his genius, he saw the truth, and expressed it in worthy forms, for these men especially share and need the feminine principle. The divine birds need to be brooded into life and song by mothers."*

If, like Asmodeus, one had the power to remove the roofs of human habitations, and take a look into the private lives and histories of some families, one might find many curious cases of special retribution, many evidences of cause and effect in the moral, as well as the physical aspect of affairs. Many an avenging Nemesis would be found at her post scourging the offender, whether in the person of the husband and father, or of the wife and mother. So long as the husband will not recognize the supreme power of his wife over the ante-natal life (both mental and physical) of her child, and give her the best possible conditions to improve it, so long will this avenging scourge hang over his head, so long will his children prove a curse instead of a blessing to his hearth-stone. So long, too, as the mother ignores her responsibility in regard to the constitution and moral nature of her expected child, and consults only her own ease and inclinations, irrespective of the laws of transmission, and feels that she has no higher function to perform than the mere involuntary instincts of animal life, that she has no exalted nature in herself to impart, so long will she impede human progress, and be the mother of a degenerate offspring.

* See Appendix H.

CHAPTER EIGHTEENTH.

A HIGHLY nervous susceptibility is one of the distinguishing attributes of woman. Through this wisely bestowed organism she is able to recognize truth as by intuition. Discarding the slow process of reasoning from facts, so necessary to man in forming his opinions, she arrives at conclusions by an apparently innate light, in sympathy with the good, the true and the useful. This predominance and activity of the nervous system in woman manifests itself most forcibly in the maternal relations, constituting her an efficient agent in transmitting strongly marked characteristics to offspring. It not unfrequently endows her with almost superhuman energy to support, to train and to educate them for good and efficient members of society. Yet, as every human function is liable to abuse or perversion, so this one, although instituted by divine wisdom to beautify and to elevate the race, may become the means of much evil, through the thoughtlessnes, selfishness, or the ignorance of herself, or of those with whom she associates.

The preceding remarks may be illustrated by the following cases; the first showing the beneficial effects of unusual energy on the part of the mother in improving the character of her unborn child; the second, the baneful action of any sudden shock or painful emotion which tends to diminish the nervous energy and strength of the mother during the period referred to; the third, the pernicious influence of distasteful associations and constant annoyance.

A lady, with whom the writer is intimate, accompanied her husband to London, where business detained him a year. At the end of that period, she returned home with another child added to her family. On being asked in regard to what she had seen in the great metropolis, she answered, not so much as she had desired; yet probably would not have seen anything of interest, had she not exerted unwonted energy and perseverance. Her husband could not attend her on account of press of business; so, thinking she might never have another opportunity to see the sights of London, she took her little son for an escort. By this means she visited every place of historic interest to which she could gain admittance, cultivated her taste for painting and sculpture in the art galleries, enlarged her knowledge of the antique in the British Museum, expanded her views in many things, and returned home with added strength of character and self-reliance as the fruits of her year's observation and experience abroad. Twenty years have elapsed, and the daughter nurtured and born under such favorable influences promises to make herself a name in the world of art. Endowed with capacity, energy and talent, she asks no questions as to woman's sphere, but feels perfectly competent to attain an independence by her own efforts. "To be weak," says Carlyle, "is to be miserable." This girl is perfectly joyous and jubilant in the plenitude of her powers, mental and physical. By what standard of money value could such advantages be computed.

This fact came to my knowledge through a friend, who was intimate with the teacher of the unfortunate child.

A young mother, within two or three months of accouchement, was thrown into a state of stupor or or syncope by sudden fright, at seeing her husband fall in convulsions at her feet. For some length of time after his recovery, she was unable to shake off the torpor and chill which had seized her, and was subject to a sensation of numbness whenever he was absent from her for any length of time. This unnatural and painful condition of the mother must have had the effect of arresting the development of her child; for when born it was unusually small and feeble, with scarcely strength enough to breathe. At ten years of age this blighted girl is diminutive in stature and idiotic in mind—not from any malformation of the brain but from the absence of nervous energy. This case was not the result of accident, or of causes unforeseen, and therefore unavoidable. The father, although an educated physician, was a gourmand, and through this habit was subject to violent convulsive attacks: the one which paralyzed his young wife, and thereby doomed his unborn daughter to idiocy was induced by a hearty supper of stewed clams!

. The late Mrs. Williamson, wife of a clergyman, and

principal of a female seminary in this city, gave me the following fact:—

"Born to affluence, my sister, Mrs B., was accustomed to the refinements of the best society, to the intellectual resources and to the social pleasures of a city life. All these advantages she enjoyed several years after her marriage, until a reverse of circumstances and a numerous family made it necessary to retrench expenses. To that end, her husband removed his family to a country residence a convenient distance from town, where he could return home every day after business hours. This change was satisfactory and agreeable to all the family during the summer months; but when inclement weather and the long winter evenings came, and my sister was left alone by the absence of her husband, night after night, with no companionship except young children, this mode of life became extremely irksome, and she grew nervous and discontented. Besides her other causes of dissatisfaction, she was annoyed by an awkward, ugly nurse-maid, who was scarcely ever out of her sight—added to all this, she had an unwelcome maternity in prospect. The child nurtured and born under such impressions and influences was extremely peevish and unhappy in disposition, and although it resembled the father in complexion and features, it appeared to have been marked through the mother's imagination with the uncouth form and the awkward manners of the disagreeable nurse-maid. So apparent was this, that before two years of age she had acquired the nickname of 'little Bridget.' Unlike all the children who preceded her, who are refined and beautiful, she is a living witness to the susceptibility of the mother during the period of gestation."

The peculiar susceptibility of the mother appears to act morally as well as intellectually and physically upon the ante-natal life of her child. A lady who had been a governess in the family of a wealthy Southern planter, gave me this fact.

The oldest daughter of the family had been persuaded by her parents, much against her own inclinations, to marry a man she did not love. She possessed a most affectionate disposition, and was ardently attached to her parents, sisters, and home. Immediately after her marriage, notwithstanding her expressed desire to remain with her family, her husband insisted upon her accompanying him to Europe. They were absent over a year, during which time a daughter was born to them. This child, nurtured on such discordant sentiments, manifested a great dislike to her father at an early age. This feeling seemed to have gained strength with her years. At the age of eight it amounted to a passion of perfect hatred ; she would never allow him to caress her without a struggle of opposition. Moreover, she sought every opportunity to keep out of his presence ; and although violent and uncontrollable with him, towards her grand-parents, whom she tenderly loved, she was gentle, docile, and tractable.

There is a useful moral to be inferred from this case, over which every overbearing husband or father should ponder well ; it may serve as a key to solve many a domestic problem—for such *Lusus Naturæ* appear not without a cause.

CHAPTER NINETEENTH.

I AM aware that in the treatment of subjects of this nature, facts are far more satisfactory than arguments. The following was related to me by a friend who had taught school in Illinois:

Among my scholars there were five belonging to one family, whose ages ranged from eight to sixteen. The two eldest were dull, inert, and slow to learn—while the third, a girl about twelve years of age, was remarkably bright, sensitive and talented. Not only apt and quick at her lessons, she possessed a fine poetic temperament, accompanied by a keen appreciation of the beauties of Nature; she could also write a theme in prose or verse with ease and facility. The children younger than Sarah were both physically and mentally superior to the two eldest, but far inferior to her in talent and refinement of manners. The cause of the great diversity of disposition and capability manifested in this family, would have continued to me an unsolved problem, had I not found a key to it in the "Parents' Guide." Therefore, in order to test its theory, and to satisfy myself on the subject, I took my sewing one Saturday afternoon, and went to visit Mrs.

Smith, the mother of this family. She was a plain, sensible woman, in capacity not above mediocrity, but self-sacrificing, and ambitious to bestow a good education on her children—characteristics peculiar to women brought up in the Eastern States. Mrs. Smith and her husband had removed to Illinois soon after their marriage, and had by their prudence and industry accumulated considerable property.

During my visit I took occasion to turn the subject of our conversation to the children. I spoke of the rare abilities of Sarah; of her affectionate and gentle disposition, of her love for reading, of her intense enjoyment of poetry, and all that was beautiful in nature, and of the advantage which she possessed over her brothers and sisters in her aptitude for acquiring knowledge. I then asked Mrs. Smith if she knew any cause to which she could attribute the rare mental gifts of this favored child.

"She did not," she replied.

Had any friend been staying with you previous to the birth of Sarah, by whose companionship and conversation your mind became interested and elevated?

"No event of that kind occurred," she answered. "The railroads were not finished in those days, traveling was expensive, and my friends and relations lived at a distance."

Can you not recollect any unusual event that transpired about the time to which I allude, that might have produced a change in your mode of life, or habits of thought?

"I cannot; my life since we settled in Illinois has been extremely monotonous—hard work, without change or recreation; for to a farmer's wife each day brings its imperative labor that cannot be evaded. But thank heaven, our children will reap the benefit of our toil and privation."

Not obtaining any satisfaction on the subject that occupied my thoughts, I gave up the inquiry for the time, determined to get at the truth by some less direct method. So after a while I turned the conversation to books and reading, and asked her if she did not consider it a great privation to be unable to procure some of the new books and periodicals, from which she might learn how much the world was progressing?

"Yes," she answered; "when we first settled here I missed my former privileges in regard to books; our friends at the East occasionally sent us newspapers, but they were not as satisfying as a good book, more especially as a book of poems would have been, for at times I feared my mind was becoming lethargic for the want of a stimulus to the imagination."

Ah! you are fond of poetry then; have you not been able to get any of your favorite reading since you came to Illinois?

"Only once; a pedlar came along late one afternoon, and asked the privilege of putting up with us for the night. After supper he brought from his wagon some books for our inspection; among them, one beautifully bound in red and gold attracted my attention. I read a few pages, was enchanted, and made up my mind that come what would, I must have the book. So not having money enough to purchase it, I walked four miles that night before bed-time in order to borrow the price of it from a neighbor."

What, may I ask, was the name of the book which you could take so much trouble to possess?

"It was the Poems of Walter Scott; and a glorious time I had in reading it, for often in the perusal of its pages I forgot my fatigues and cares."

How long since did this event occur, Mrs. Smith?

"Oh, I do not remember; a long time ago. But now I do remember—it was some months before Sarah was born; because having read it so often I knew much of it by rote, and used to sing the songs to her when she was a baby, and repeat the stories to her when she was a little girl."

Ah, indeed! why, this may account for her love of poetry and imaginative turn of mind.

"It may, but I never thought of it before in that light."

Parents, I answered, are generally over-anxious to accumulate property in order to enrich their children. But do you not think that children would prefer a sound physical constitution, and a good mental development, to great worldly possessions without them?

"Yes indeed, for I am sure that our two eldest boys would give all their father's farm, if they owned it, in exchange for Sarah's good health, cheerful disposition, and fine mental qualities."

Mr. Smith understands, I have heard, and puts in practice all the new methods by which the live stock on his farm can be improved. Did it never occur to him that the same laws which govern the improvement of domestic animals, might with equal advantage be applied to the human species?

"I don't understand you."

For instance, he knows that in order to secure a strong, active and finely developed colt, he must be careful of the mare; must not work her too much, must give her good food, a clean and well ventilated stable, and exercise sufficient to keep her in an active and lively condition.

"That is true; and I now wonder that men have never thought of putting in practice, in their own families, the knowledge they have obtained on this subject. Your suggestion, madam, has stirred up the fountain of memory, and caused a new light to dawn on my mind—for I now think that if, during the period of gestation with my first children, my work had been less exhausting, and my mental faculties more exercised, they might have been born with stronger constitutions and more active minds."

There is not a doubt of that in my mind, but has it never occurred to you that woman is the only created being that is liable and often necessitated to labor beyond her strength during the period of which we are speaking. Nature, however, is a good accountant, and never allows herself to be defrauded; the parent who is blind to her behests in this regard, will never experience the exquisite pleasure of feeling proud of his children.

CHAPTER TWENTIETH.

It is a common saying with superficial observers, that marriage is a lottery, in which the chances are about equal for blanks or prizes; and also, that the moral and intellectual capability of children cannot be predicted with any degree of certainty; as their good or evil qualities, are the effects of causes, over which the parents have no control.

Here is an instance of the fallacy of such unsound opinions.

A young married lady became much interested in the, to her, new views on human progress, disclosed in the "Parents' Guide to the Transmission of Intellectual and Moral Qualities." Its facts and arguments appeared reasonable and logical; its theory philosophical and beautiful; and she thanked God for the privilege of testing its truths. Therefore, from the earliest period of her hopes of maternity, she kept her Divine Mission in view, and governed herself accordingly She endeavored to cultivate a cheerful disposition,—to indulge in no sentiments that were unkind or uncharitable,—to keep out of the way of all unpleasant sights or sounds,—to subdue nervous irritability, and impatience,—to fill her mind with images of grace and beauty,—to live in harmony with all her surroundings, —and then leave the rest to God. With His blessing on her efforts, she could with confidence look forward to her reward, in the birth of a new Immortal, that should bear witness to the truths of His Divinely instituted laws of human progress. Nor was she disappointed ; for this child is, at the age of five years, all that a cultivated, refined, and affectionate mother could desire. Bright, active, and intelligent,—beautiful, pure, and innocent as an angel, he promises to become the pride, as he is now the joy of his parents. His future good conduct can be confidently relied on, —more especially, as his parents come of good stock, and have improved the advantages of a superior education. High mental culture, therefore, will be of easy acquisition by their son.

There is a saying among the ancients, that, "Whom the gods love die young." There may be more significance in this, than meets the eye. According to the popular belief of the ancients those whom the gods loved, they endowed with genius,—with mental and physical graces which are generally manifested through a delicately sensitive organization. Now it is well known that children thus constituted, are more susceptible to surrounding influences, than those in whom the animal and vital nature predominate ; hence, they would be most likely to die young. There are, it is well known, many medicinal remedies, and some common articles of food, that may be given with impunity to the children of the laboring classes, in whom the nervous system is subordinate to the vital,—but which would destroy those whose parents had transmitted to them a finely susceptible organization. Doubtless many children of the latter class, (to which the gifted one above referred to belongs,) are daily sacrificed to a want of knowledge on this subject. Not until some preparation for parenthood is made indispensible to the education of youth, will this "Slaughter of the Innocents" cease![*]

A friend related to me to the following instance of a remarkable musical genius, which was not inherited, but produced by the influence of music upon the imagination of the mother, during the period of gestation.

A sister-in-law of my husband, whom I had never before seen, came from St. Louis to make us a visit. She brought with her a little daughter about five years of age, who possessed a most extraordinary talent for music. She would run her fingers over the keys of the piano, and produce the sweetest harmony, which, when accompanied by her voice might move the heart of a stoic, by its tender sensibility. Knowing that this talent had not been inherited from the father, or any of his family, I asked the mother if she herself was a proficient in music.

"I am not," she replied, "but I believe that I impressed the child before she was born, with this speciality. During the whole period of gestation, I occupied appartments adjoining those of a lady who taught music, and was in the habit of singing and playing every day. This constant practice, however, annoyed

---

[*] See Appendix G.

some of the other inmates, who made many efforts to have her removed from the house; they endeavored to persuade me to join them,—saying if I made a complaint, she would surely have to leave. This I declined, for the reasons, that being among strangers, and my husband much from home, I frequently felt lonely and low spirited,—the music cheered and harmonized my mind; and because her own support, and that of an infirm mother depended upon her respectable position and success as a teacher. So instead of joining in that persecution, I made use of my influence to have her remain in the house; and God has rewarded me, by bestowing upon my child the talents which I admired and protected in my neighbor."

"Nor is this all," she continued, "I believe that the firmness exercised by me on that occasion, tended to engender in the mind of my unborn child, a persistency of purpose that will be beneficial to her through life. For I should like to see the person who could induce her to relinquish that which she thought to be right, and just,—or to do anything that her conscience did not approve."

CHAPTER TWENTY-FIRST.

Mrs. Shelly's Frankenstein might be considered an Allegory, typifying moral and intellectual monstrosities of human creation. But if the parent could not, as in the case of Frankenstein, shake off or get away from the presence of the degraded being to whom he had given existence, there would doubtless have been a less number of monsters in human form brought into the world, to become a terror or a burden to society.

The preceding reflection was suggested by a visit to the House of Refuge. The dishonest propensities of some of the inmates of this institution appear to be so thoroughly innate, that they are considered irreclaimable. Now this moral obliquity which has blighted their lives, should awaken in us only sentiments of pity and commiseration. For if the conduct and habits of the parents previous to, and during the ante-natal lives of the children, could be known, it would be found in many instances that they had been more sinned against than sinning.

The following case will illustrate this view of the subject.

Some years since a friend of the writer had in her employ a man-servant, who was much above his class in point of ability and education. His only fault appeared to spring from an over-active organ of acquisitiveness. The inconvenience arising from this spirit of greed was overlooked in consideration of his desirable qualifications as a butler. His wife, who was as avaricious as himself, kept house in the neighborhood—and it was well known derived her support from the store-room of the family. So long as the pilfering was confined to the mere necessaries of life, it was allowed to pass unnoticed. But when it was discovered that the man had betrayed the confidence reposed in him, and abstracted the most expensive wines from the cellar, as well as the delicacies of the larder, he was dismissed from his situation. During the many months in which this woman was luxuriating on the fruits of theft, and assisting her husband in his petty larcenies, she was transmitting thieving propensities to her unborn child. The result has proved that if the parents had deliberately designed to produce a dishonest offspring, they practised the most certain method to accomplish that end; for all the native acuteness of intellect which this child possesses is directed to dishonest purposes.

The catalogue of books on the transmission of tendencies to physical diseases, would fill a volume—whilst those on the transmission of intellectual and moral maladies might be counted on the fingers, and are to be found principally in the reports of asylums and prisons. Occasionally, however, these truths are recognized by the best novelists of the day

—and sometimes appear to be incidentally thrown out amongst the Oriental pearls of Emerson, Holmes, and other wise men of the East.

There are well known instances of the children of apparently worthy parents, who early manifest a vicious and depraved disposition. These anomalies, according to the teachings of modern theology, are attributed to the doctrine of original sin ; but tested by the ever operative laws of cause and effect, they no longer remain enigmas. The following text of Scripture may indicate a solution of some of these " dispensations of a mysterious Providence"—" Be sure your sin will find you out."

Here is a case in point, the counterpart of which may be found within the circle of many persons' acquaintance.

A young gentleman, who possessed a good understanding, and superior business qualifications, in his haste to become rich, allowed himself to be influenced in his choice of a wife by motives of worldly interest. Not possessing a high standard of female excellence, nor any knowledge of the laws of hereditary descent, he paid no attention to the characteristics, or to the antecedents, of the family to which he allied himself. Considering the transaction from a mercantile standpoint, he was satisfied that he had made a profitable investment of himself,—for his wife brought him wealth, position and influence, together with several other matters of minor importance, in the estimation of the worldly-minded,—such as a feeble organization, a predisposition to hereditary insanity,—and children, who manifested at an early age decided proclivities to vice and sensuality. The existence of one of their sons dated from a period of his father's life, marked by a rail-road speculation, in which he succeeded in transferring the property of the widow and the orphan to his own overflowing coffers. Another son was born to him soon after a commercial panic, of which he availed himself, to stop payment, and buy up his liabilities at one-half their value. By this financial swindle, he doubled his capital, without injuring his reputation much, in the estimation of those who rate success in business, above integrity of character, or high moral principle. During the flood-tide of his prosperity, when he thought the world was made for his especial enjoyment, and indulged himself in every sensual pleasure, a daughter was born to him, who inherited her mother's weak intellect, and her father's strong propensities. Thus unfortunately constituted, she has to be kept under strict surveillance, and has not yet found an opportunity to elope with a married man, nor to marry her father's coachman.

This father had, owing to an occasional inward glance, or to the recollections of his own early experience, formed a low estimate of youthful virtue. Therefore, in order to shield his sons from the temptations to which they would have been exposed in a large city, he sent them to one of the best institutions of learning, which the country afforded; hoping, thereby to qualify them to enter one of the learned professions. But his ambitious hopes were doomed to bitter disappointment; for his sons were found incapable, both mentally, and physically, of receiving a liberal education,—and their subsequent conduct has made manifest the truth of the text, for the sins of the father have found him out.

The tendency to fraud, untruthfulness, and deception, appears also to be trnsmitted. Who cannot mention whole families of his acquaintance, whose veracity must be taken at a discount? We talk of vice which runs in the blood,—certainly, when the fountain is corrupt, all the streams are more or less impure. "When the fathers have eaten sour grapes, the children's teeth are set on edge."

A young couple, previous to their marriage, were suspected of improper relations. The imputation was strenuously denied by the wife, who for several months subsequent to the union persisted in falsehood and prevarication in order to conceal her error. This evil habit not only stultified her own soul, but deeply tainted the young life that was drawing its being from her own. Her unfortunate son, born a few months after marriage, has now reached the age of manhood —but the confirmed habit of falsifying seems to have become a part of his nature. His word can never be trusted—it appears a passion with him to prevaricate, to mis-state the simplest occurrence, and never to be straight-forward, frank, or open in any thing that he says or does. He is also extremely sensitive—is wounded to the quick by any exposure of his duplicity, so that his friends are forced to be constantly on their guard in order to save his feelings, and to prevent an almost insane suffering. His mother's family look upon this affliction as a Divine judgment visited upon guilty parents. It has brought bitter sorrow to the household; and younger brothers and sisters, who are evenly balanced in mind and upright in character, cannot remove the grief caused by the unfortunate organization of their eldest son.

A woman who had inherited an unconquerable propensity to theft, was able to restrain the passion to a great degree; yet there were times when she seemed overcome by her weakness as by a species of insanity. Trading in a store where various articles were spread before her, she could not resist the temptation to pilfer a roll of tape, or a paper of pins; yet she was in easy circumstances, and afterwards heartily ashamed—despising herself for her meanness and guilt. She educated her children in habits of strict honesty, endeavoring to impress upon their minds a horror of theft. Although their father was a man of unimpeachable honesty and integrity, yet this tendency to the monomania of stealing descended as a most powerful instinct to several of her children. One of them acknowledged that there were times when she could not go into the parlor of a friend without the thought crossing her mind—how easy it would be to secrete some of the ornaments in the room,—that the very thought of such meanness was extremely repulsive to her, yet she could not prevent its recurrence. This tendency, in various forms, had tortured her more or less all through life; yet she was too high-minded to yield to such degrading suggestions. She justly regarded it as a fatal hereditary weakness, which could only be overcome by successive generations of integrity of conduct.

This is not an isolated case. The tendency to petty larceny among women of even great respectability is often remarked by merchants. It is considered much less safe to trust them with a variety of small merchandise than it is to trust men. The latter have other ways and opportunities of overreaching and defrauding, but women have little business dealings outside of their own families, except in shopping. A merchant told me that some of his best lady-customers had from time to time been seen to take small articles secretly, yet he dared not think of speaking of it, as it would ruin his business, and create scandal unnecessarily. Every now and then some case of this kind is dragged before the public, to the bitter mortification of friends and relatives.

Recently I have come to regard this light-fingered tendency among the lovers of shopping as a species of moral mania. A mother who has yielded to its humiliating influence is almost certain to leave the instinct in the same direction, impressed upon her child. Then like circumstances produce a like vice.

CHAPTER TWENTY-SECOND.

In the first part of this work, published twenty years ago, examples were given of various remarkable persons who inherited their strong mental traits from the mother. I am now able to cite other examples in which hereditary intellectual qualities have descended directly from the father. Probably as many instances can be adduced on the one side as on the other.— Doubtless in every instance it will be found that the peculiarities of both parents were merged in the child, each contributing to the rare combination of the new being.

Blaise Pascal, "perhaps the most brilliant intellect that ever lighted on this lower world," was the son of a French savan. His father was one of the finest scholars, and especially one of the best mathematicians of his time—and the splendid gifts of the son seemed like a direct inheritance from the sire.

Young Pascal lost his mother at a very early age. We know very little of her. Few women at that period were eminent in history. But we are told that she was descended from the best families in the province of Auvergne, on the side of both father and mother. A long line of cultivated ancestry was needed to perfect this wonderful child.

From early childhood young Pascal's brilliant mental powers were the admiration of the age. Unfortunately, however, from the effect of intense application, his health failed before he arrived at manhood, and after a life of pain and suffering, he died at the early age of thirty-six. Pity there were none to teach him the laws of life and health! "The murder of the Innocents" has always been countenanced by admiring friends, as well as by a perverted public sentiment.

Another instance in which a special talent appears to have descended directly from the father, may be found in the Bonheur family of France.

Rosa Bonheur, by her pre-eminent genius, has made her name a household word in all civilized countries. She has, however, two brothers—one a sculptor and the other a painter—who have already obtained much celebrity as artists, and also a sister who superintends the Free School of Design for Girls in Paris.

The father of this gifted family was himself an artist, and although neither great in art, nor wealthy nor successful, yet he has transmitted his own talents increased many-fold to his children.

We are told that the genius of the Bonheurs was derived from the father, and this was supposed to be the end of the matter. No one speaks of the mother; one cannot learn any thing of her or of her history.— Yet the laws of mental inheritance are sufficiently established to enable us to venture the assertion that the mother, too, must have been a woman of fine powers, of fine qualities of temperament, which combining with the talents of the father, have re-appeared in the children and given them genius.

We have an illustration of this at home, in our great family of marked and rather eccentric geniuses, the Beechers. They are all most unmistakably 'chips of the old block.' The grain and fiber of Beecherism is in every one of them. Yet the children of the first mother differ from those of the last; and the two most popular and brilliant members of the family—Stowe, and Henry Ward—were born when their parents were in the fullest maturity, use, and confidence of their powers.

The late Theodore Parker is another example of strong and sturdy manhood, inherited from a like ancestry. He was descended in a direct line from the Puritan settlers of the Massachusetts colony; his ancestors, almost without exception, having been farmers and mechanics, and usually active participants in the military affairs of their day. His grandfather, John Parker, was a zealous friend of liberty, and was captain in the battle of Lexington. His father was a millwright and pump-maker, a man of robust habits and sturdy sense, a great reader, fond of mathematics, with which branch of science he was well acquainted—an independent thinker—a Unitarian in belief, and possessing remarkable powers of expression and argument. His mother was a highly cultivated woman for that day—a model of personal beauty, fond of literature, and with an enthusiastic taste for poetry.

Here was the son of many brave and hardy generations, reproducing and intensifying in himself the marked family traits. Here also is another victim of violated law. It is said that he was accustomed to the most prolonged study, sometimes averaging fifteen hours a day—study too of the most exhaustive kind, varied by fatiguing journeys to lecture; add to this the effort of speaking every Sunday in an immense hall—no wonder that he died at fifty, though he ought to have lived to eighty.

John Quincy Adams was probably the most remarkable instance of transmitted mental traits of character to be found in the annals of this country. The following extract from the life of his father, John Adams, abundantly proves to what extent his great intellectual powers and his unimpeachable moral integrity were a direct inheritance.

"In two things* he was favored above most men who have lived. He was happily married to a woman whose character was singularly fitted to develope every good trait of his own; with a mind capable of comprehending his, with affection strong enough to respond to his sensibility, with a sympathy equal to his highest aspirations, and yet with flexibility enough to yield to his stronger will without impairing her own dignity. In this blessed relation he was permitted to continue fifty-four years, embracing more than the whole period of his active life; and it is not too much to say that to it he was indebted not merely for the domestic happiness which ran so like a thread of silver through the most troubled current of his days, but for the steady and unwavering support of all the high-

---

* Says his biographer, Charles Adams, the talented son of John Quincy Adams.

est purposes of his career. Upon the several occasions when his action placed him in the most critical and difficult positions, when the popular voice seemed loud in condemning the wisdom or the patriotism of his course, her confidence in his correctness seemed never to have wavered for a moment. Not a trace of hesitation or doubt is to be seen in her most confidential communications; on the contrary, her voice in those cases came in to reinforce his determinations, and to urge him to persevere. Often she is found to have drawn her conclusions in advance; for several of her letters bear on the outside the testimony of her husband's admiration of her sagacity. The soothing effect this must have had upon him when chafed as his temper frequently was by the severe friction to which it was exposed in the great struggles of his life, may easily be conceived. An ignoble spirit would have thrown him into depression; a repining and dissatisfied one would have driven him frantic. Hers was lofty, yet cheerful; decided, yet gentle. Whilst she understood the foibles of his character and yielded enough to maintain her own proper authority, she never swerved from her admiration of his abilities, her reliance upon the profoundness of his judgment, and her pride in the integrity of his life. And if this was her state of feeling, it was met on his part by a devotion which never wavered, and a confidence scarcely limited by a doubt of the possibility of an error. A domestic relation like this compensated for all that was painful and afflictive in the vicissitudes of his career; and its continuance to so late a stage in their joint lives left to the survivor little further to wish for in this world beyond the hope of a reunion in the next.

"The other extraordinary blessing was the possession of a son, who fulfilled in his career all the most sanguine expectations of a father. From his earliest youth John Quincy Adams had given symptoms of uncommon promise, and contrary to what so frequently happens in such cases, every year as it passed over his head only tended the more to confirm the hopes that had been raised from the beginning. A friendly nature received from early opportunities of travel and instruction in foreign lands, not the noxious seeds which so often germinate to spread corruption, but a generous and noble development as well of the intellect as of the affections. At twenty years of age his father saw in him the outline of a full grown statesman, a judgment which time served only the more unequivocally to confirm. But it was not merely in the circumstances of his brilliant progress as a public man that his parents had reason to delight. As a son affectionate, devoted and pure, his parents never failed to find in him sources of the most unmingled satisfaction. In whatever situation he was placed, and however far removed from them in the performance of his duties, he never forgot the obligation he owed to soothe by every effort in his power the hours of their declining years. The voluminous correspondence which was the offspring of this relation furnishes an affecting proof of the tenderness and devotion of the son to his parents, and of their implicit trust and grateful pride in their child. And the pleasure was reserved to the father, rarely enjoyed since time began, of seeing his son gradually forcing his way by his own unaided abilities, up the steps of the same ascent where he had stood before him, until he reached the last and highest which his country could supply. The case is unexampled in popular goverments. And when this event was fully accomplished, whilst the son was yet in the full enjoyment of his great dignity so honorably acquired, it was accorded the old patriarch to go to his rest on the day alone, of all the days in the year, which was the most imperishably associated with his fame. Such things are not often read of, even in the most gorgeous pictures of mortal felicity painted in Eastern story. They go far to relieve the darker shadows which fly over the ordinary paths of life, and to hold out the hope that even under the present imperfect dispensation, it is not unreasonable to trust that virtue may meet with its just reward."

CHAPTER TWENTY-THIRD.

Dr. Laycock in his work on "Mind and Brain," says, "M. L'Abbé Frère Cannor, of the Cathedral of Paris, has lately formed a collection of ancient skulls sent to him from all parts of Europe; and has deduced from a comparison of them, the general conclusion, that in proportion as the skulls belonged to an ancient and primitive race, in the same proportion the frontal region is flattened and the occipital developed. Such a conclusion if verified, would go far to establish the general law, that each of the successive generations of men adds something, however small, to the evolutions of the human mind; and that amidst all the struggle of the races, and the decay of inferior tribes, a higher and nobler type of humanity is more and more developed."

According to this conclusion, it follows, that if the son of many generations of highly educated ancestors, dies without leaving descendants, all the accumulated capability up to him is lost to the world, and he defrauds the state of one of its most precious treasures, the continuation of the line of an improved race.

If the sons of cultivated ancestors ought to marry

in order to leave descendants for the good of their country—then why is not the same obligation in force in regard to the daughters? The number of women of this class who remain single is much greater than that of the men. In the present state of fashionable society, superior intellectual culture or power, is no recommendation to candidates for matrimony, if unaccompanied by wealth or high connection. Although it is a well established fact, that great men have almost invariably been the sons of able mothers,* yet the most gifted and capable women are frequently left in a state of celibacy.

If, as the poet says, " a bold peasantry's their country's pride," then how infinitely more proud should a nation be of a population in which the moral and intellectual elements preponderate even among the laboring classes.† Washington, Franklin, Adams, and a host of other great men, are the models on which our national character has been moulded,—the lever by which it has been elevated to its present position among the nations of the earth,—where, when this cup shall have passed away, it will stand, a haven to the

---

* " The mother of John and Charles Wesley—like so many mothers of eminent men—was remarkable for strong sense, high principle, deep piety, uncommon natural talent, energy, and force of character. It is easy to prophesy after the event; but one feels disposed to say, that the sons of such a woman could hardly turn out mere ordinary men."
—North British Review, Feb. 1860.

† It must be borne in mind, that one of the causes of the unusual mental activity which characterizes the American people, may be ascribed to their constant mixture with other nations.

oppressed, and a warning to the oppressor,—where the magnificent problem of the practicability of self-government of an enlightened people shall be successfully demonstrated, and the rights of humanity vindicated,—and where the operation the democratic principle will no longer be considered an experiment, but a brilliant success.

In the course of human progress it will indubitably become manifest, that a nation's wealth must be placed upon a more elevated basis than material interest. As humanity stands at the head of all else,—so must the political economist measure a nation's prosperity and stability, by its high standard of morality, both individually and collectively,—by its inherited tendencies to intellectual culture,—by its consequent refinement of manners, and advanced civilization,—and by its self-sacrificing efforts to succor the oppressed, and to elevate, and strengthen, the *weak and the lowly.*

Esquirol, one of the most profound writers that France ever produced, remarks, "that children whose existence dated from the horrors of the first French Revolution turned out to be weak, nervous, and irritable in mind, extremely susceptible, and liable to be thrown by the least extraordinary excitement into absolute insanity."

Such a result of maternity, performed under such circumstances, would be predicable to any mind sufficiently enlightened in natural laws, to appreciate the mother's office, and its influence for good or evil on her child. These facts give proof of what would have been regarded seventy-five years ago, even by the most enlightened, as mere *hypothesis,* and by those of average intelligence as insane or atheistic speculation. It is now well known that the Creator is not chargeable with the idiots and the imbeciles,—few persons in our country at least, are yet dark enough to suppose that He punishes one human being by creating another, subject to the most fearful infirmities that can afflict humanity; hence we are willing to acknowledge facts which we were wont to lay at His door, as the results of our own conduct and conditions.

Great emotional influences brought to bear on a generation, will leave their consequences in good as well as in evil,—in power as well as in weakness,—in capacity for noble purposes, as well as incapacity, feebleness, and the conditions named by the French philosopher. Looked at from this point of view, the American nation has something noble to expect, from its education of mothers, within the last twenty years, on the slavery question. The discussions which have taken place showing its wrongs and its horrors,—the preparation which it has received through those discussions, to pass into dramatic form, and so seize upon woman's compassionate feelings, her inate sense of justice, by its vivid strictures of outraged humanity. The excitement produced by the publication of "Uncle Tom's Cabin," and the various anti-slavery novels which followed it in quick succession, have furnished ground whereon to predicate the downfall of American slavery, when the generations born under their powerful appeals shall live and move the nation.

Such experiences can no more be lost than seed sown in good soil can fail to return in due time. Nature forbids this waste; and, whether we know it or not, they come back to us augmented in force, as the crop from the sower's grain. The complaint now is, that we have no men equal to the great emergency in which the nation finds itself. We are too far removed from the period of any really noble struggle. The men born of the Revolutionary times have passed away, and we have only such as sprang into life under the influences of prosperity and comfort that left the maternal powers stagnant, or worse, that pampered them with ease and luxury, making self-indulgence, rather than self-denial, the law of maternal life. We cannot have noble men or a noble people, unless the mothers of our nation are moved to noble purposes by something within or something without themselves that is adequate to that end.

There is no greater fallacy than the common belief that circumstances make great men, although advanced by the first Napoleon. Circumstances are all-important, but they must date back to the origin of life, as in his case. Circumstance is often *opportunity* to men, but the man of capacity must be there, waiting for the opportunity. No combination of circumstances can make heroes of cowards, magnanimous men of self-seekers, nor patriots of those whose self-interest overrules all love of country or feelings of humanity. Opportunity only opens the way backward to such men; they block the way of the car of progress, instead of lending aid to its forward movement.

The *great generations* appear as the fruit of a generous or earnest struggle for right among the nations where the mind of woman is sufficiently developed to be a party in the struggle—as in the American Revolution, that also of the Dutch, so ably treated by Mr. Motley, who recognizes the woman's share in that fearful history, and to that of the French Revolution, already referred to. There must, however, be a moral character to the struggle in order to produce its best effects on women; for according to Esquerol, mere bloodshed and horrors will reappear in feebleness and unsoundness in the succeeding generation; but if the spirit manifested in the struggle be that of injustice and selfishness, then it may be a harvest from the dragon's teeth, such as we feel that England is sowing to-day to reap in humiliation hereafter. For our corn-laden Griswold she sent us her piratical crafts the Alabama and the Florida—acts for which she will find it difficult to escape "the coals of juniper and the arrows of the mighty"! When the oligarchs of England find themselves powerless before those who rise up against them, the nation may remember and become wiser by recollection that in our present struggle for an undivided nationality, she, recreant to her former principles, actually gave herself to a band of Iscariot desecrators of, and dealers in humanity. The mothers of her arrogant and privileged classes fold their robes about them and sit down in ease and indifference to-day—their children will do likewise; but the mothers of the *people*, whose hearts throb at the mention of America (their land of promise), and beat more quickly on the receipt of good or bad news of our war, will reap the harvest of progress that will bless themselves and elevate their class to the *true* Christian standard of national character in the coming ages.

CHAPTER TWENTY-FOURTH.

NOVELTIES are always more or less attractive, because they lead to new thoughts or fresh sensations. When, however, we meet a novel theory, which is likely to excite discussion among earnest men—to quicken observation in many departments of natural science, and to stimulate anew to widely different investigations among the most learned, we can but hail it with rejoicing. True or false, it is the precursor to the discovery of more enlarged truth.

These thoughts have been suggested by the recent work of Darwin on the "Origin of Species." If the positions taken are not altogether new, yet they are for the first time stated upon the authority of a careful scientific basis, in a connected and well considered form, by one widely and favorably known in the scientific world. The writer has thrown down his gauntlet —an elaborate argument, already sustained by many facts, and to be hereafter fortified, as he assures us, by an immense body of testimony which he has been for years carefully collecting, and which he thinks to an unprejudiced mind must be abundantly satisfactory. As his main position would overthrow the established creed of all leading naturalists, they of course must accept his challenge, and come to the rescue of their ancient landmarks. Hence, even though Darwin may have given to the world nothing but a splendid hypothesis, which shall prove hereafter to be unsustained by facts, yet all science will doubtless be benefited by the new impetus which he has given to investigation. It is refreshing to find any one who dares to think boldly, originally, and yet conscientiously in any direction.

But leaving the wise naturalists, who have devoted a lifetime to the subject, to settle among themselves the intricate problem of the "Origin of Species," let us briefly refer to a few of Darwin's positions, bearing more especially upon topics kindred with those which we have already considered in the present volume.

If we are the lineal descendants of the fishes, at any rate they are ancestors so remote that we have lost much of our sympathy for those cold-blooded progenitors. Our nearer kinsfolk can interest us more readily; and we can more intelligently, perhaps more profitably, consider the thousand related influences which render our natures kindred with theirs.

Whether or not our author has really proved that species are only varieties, further developed by natural selection into sufficient diversity of organism to be classed apart, and thus afterwards regarded each as a separate creation, may be a question. Agassiz will tell us that he has proved nothing of the kind; and I leave the ground where learned doctors are so vigorously disagreeing, to consider merely the diversity of individuals and of varieties (considered as such) and their causes. Here there is common ground, and the testimony of a careful observer may be of value.

"When we look to the individuals of the same variety or sub-variety," says Darwin,* "of our older cultivated plants and animals, one of the first points which strikes us, is, that they generally differ much more from each other, than do the individuals of any one species or variety in a state of nature. When we reflect on the vast diversity of the plants and animals which have been cultivated, and which have varied during all ages under the most different climates and treatment, I think we are driven to conclude that this greater variability is simply due to our domestic productions having been raised under conditions of life not so uniform as, and somewhat different from, those to which the parent species have been exposed under nature. There is also, I think, some probability in the view propounded by Andrew Knight, that this variability may be partly connected with excess of food. It seems pretty clear that organic beings must be exposed during several generations to the new conditions of life to cause any appreciable amount of variation; and that when the organization has once begun to vary, it generally continues to vary for several generations. No case is on record of a variable being ceasing to be variable under cultivation. Our oldest cultivated plants, such as wheat, still often yield new varieties; our oldest domesticated animals are still capable of rapid improvement or modification.

"It has been disputed at what period of life the

* Page 14.

causes of variability, whatever they may be, generally act; whether during the early or late period of development of the embryo, or at the instant of conception. Geoffroy St. Hilaire's experiments show that unnatural treatment of the embryo causes monstrosities, and monstrosities cannot be separated by any clear line of distinction from mere variations. But I am strongly inclined to suspect that the most frequent cause of va riability may be attributed to the male and female reproductive elements having been affected prior to the act of conception. Several reasons make me believe in this; but the chief one is the remarkable effect which confinement or cultivation has on the functions of the reproductive system; this system appearing to be far more susceptible than any other part of the organization to the action of any change in the conditions of life. Nothing is more easy than to tame an animal, and few things more difficult than to get it to breed freely under confinement, even in the many cases when the male and female unite. How many animals there are which will not breed, though living long under not very close confinement in their native country! This is generally attributed to vitiated instincts; but how many cultivated plants display the utmost vigor, and yet rarely or never seed! In some few such cases it has been found out that very trifling changes, such as a little more or less water at some particular period of growth, will determine whether or not the plant sets a seed. I cannot here enter on the copious details which I have collected on this curious subject; but to show how singular the laws are which determine the reproduction of animals under confinement, I may just mention that carnivorous animals, even from the tropics, breed in this country pretty freely under confinement, with the exception of the plantigrades or bear family; whereas carnivorous birds, with the rarest exceptions, hardly ever lay fertile eggs. Many exotic plants have pollen utterly worthless, in the same exact condition as in the most sterile hybrids. When, on the one hand, we see domesticated animals and plants, though often weak and sickly, yet breeding quite freely under confinement; and when, on the other hand, we see individuals, though taken young from a state of nature, perfectly tamed, long-lived and healthy, (of which I could give numerous instances,) yet having their reproductive system so seriously affected by unperceived causes as to fail in acting. we need not be surprised at this system, when it does act under confinement, acting no' quite regularly, and producing offspring not perfectly like their parents, or variable.

"Sterility has been said to be the bane of horticulture; but on this view we owe variability to the same cause which produces sterility; and variability is the source of all the choicest productions of the garden. 1 may add, that as some organisms will breed most freely under the most unnatural conditions, (for instance, the rabbit and ferret kept in hutches,) showing that their reproductive system has not been thus affected—so will some animals and plants withstand domestication or cultivation, and vary very slightly—perhaps hardly more than in a state of nature.

"A long list could easily be given of 'sporting plants;' by this term gardeners mean a single bud or offset, which suddenly assumes a new and sometimes very different character from that of the rest of the plant. Such buds can be propagated by grafting, &c. and sometimes by seed. These 'sports' are extremely rare under nature, but far from rare under cultivation —and in this case we see that the treatment of the parent has affected a bud or offset, and not the ovules or pollen. But it is the opinion of most physiologists that there is no essential difference between a bud and an ovule in their earliest stages of formation; so that, in fact, 'sports' support my view, that variability may be largely attributed to the ovules or pollen, or to both, having been affected by the treatment of the parent prior to the act of conception. These cases anyhow show that variation is not necessarily connected, as some authors have supposed, with the act of generation."

CHAPTER TWENTY-FIFTH.

To me, there is very much in what Darwin says of the "cause of variability" as often being "prior to the act of conception." Especially in a highly-organized being like man, where the whole mental, moral, and physical constitution of both parents, and even of their progenitors, combine in the offspring, producing a marked union of characteristics, some of which are often directly traceable to each of the various ancestors. It is beyond question, that neither the state of the parents, at the time of conception, nor the condition of the mother previous to the birth, can always account for the very great diversities in the children.

I have been profoundly impressed with the fact that the whole past characters of the progenitors are transmitable, though in ever variable combinations to their descendants; and to find concurrent testimony, affirmed by science, in its observations, even in the animal and vegetable world, has much strengthened my faith in that direction.

Darwin says, "The cause may have acted, and I believe generally has acted, even before the embryo is formed; and the variation may be due to the male and female sexual elements having been affected by the conditions to which either parent or their ancestors have been exposed. Nevertheless, an effect thus caused at a very early period, even before the formation of the embryo, may appear late in life; as when a hereditary disease, which appears in old age alone, has been communicated to the offspring from the reproductive elements of one parent."* He adduces numerous evidences in proof, which are of much weight; as for example, peculiarly shaped horns in crossed breed cattle, which cannot appear until late in life, but which, when developed, resemble those of one of the parents, and proves that the peculiarity was inherited, though for years it might remain unsuspected in the young animal.

Peculiarities, tendencies, and diseases, are thus often, perhaps, generally developed late in life; although they are unquestionably hereditary, yet because the reward, or the penalty, is not early made manifest, people often refuse to believe in its existence. If there were time, and it were quite germain to the purpose, I might instance many curious facts stated by Darwin, to prove that an inherited tendency in the offspring more generally appears at about the age at which it first appeared in the parent, rather than at an earlier period of its existence; but I will merely refer to him as authority on that point, and turn to another portion of the subject.

* Page 385.

I again give his own words.* "The number and diversity of inheritable deviations of structure, both those of slight and those of considerable physiological importance is endless. Dr. Prosper Lucas's treatise in two large volumes, is the fullest and the best on this subject. No breeder doubts how strong is the tendency to inheritance: like produces like is his fundamental belief: doubts have been thrown on this principle by theoretical writers alone. When a deviation appears not unfrequently, and we see it in the father and child, we cannot tell whether it may not be due to the same original cause acting on both; but when amongst individuals apparently exposed to the same conditions, any very rare deviation due to some extraordinary combination of circumstances, appears in the parent—say once among several million individuals—and it re-appears in the child, the mere doctrine of chances almost compels us to attribute its re-appearance to inheritance. Every one must have heard of cases of albinism, prickly skin, hairy bodies, &c., appearing in several members of the same family. If strange and rare deviations of structure are truly inherited, less strange and commoner deviations may be freely admitted to be inheritable. Perhaps the correct way of viewing the whole subject would be to look at the inheritance of every character whatever as the rule, and non-inheritance as the anomaly.

"The laws governing inheritance are quite unknown; no one can say why the same peculiarity in different individuals of the same species is sometimes

* Page 18.

inherited and sometimes not so; why the child often reverts in certain characteristics to its grandfather or grandmother, or other much more remote ancestor;* why a peculiarity is often transmitted from one sex to both sexes, or to one sex alone, more commonly but, not exclusively to the like sex."

The abundant facts adduced by this writer make his opinions on these points of great weight. No two individuals are ever quite alike. Nature never repeats herself; yet she always works through means. If she tends always, as Darwin thinks, through the principle of "natural selection" to strengthen every part which can best subserve the uses of the individual, to foster the strongest, and to add to his strength, to strive continually to perfect her work, man, also, by studying her methods and co-working with her to produce similar results, may continually increase every upward

---

* One of the perturbing influences of direct inheritance, according to Mr. Lewis, is what is known as *atavism*, or ancestral influence. "This phenomenon is to be explained on the supposition that the qualities were transmitted from the grandfather to the father, in whom they were *masked* by the presence of some antagonistic or controlling influence, and thence transmitted to the son, in whom, the antagonistic influence being withdrawn, they manifest themselves. A man has a remarkable aptitude for music; but the influence of his wife is such that their children, inheriting from her imperfect ear, manifest no musical talent whatever. These children, however, have inherited the disposition of their father, in spite of its non-manifestation; and if, when they transmit what in them is latent, the influence of their wives is favorable, the grandchildren may turn out to be musically-gifted. In the same way consumption or insanity seems to lie dormant for a generation, and in the next flashes out with the same fury as of old. *Atavism* is thus a phenomenon always to be borne in mind as one of the many complications of this complex problem."

tendency, both in himself and in all *races* of men, animals and plants. This fact is of immense importance. While Nature, by herself, works slowly towards desirable ends, man, with his intelligence, by selecting the proper means, may immeasurably accelerate her work. His power in this direction, seems without limit. Here is testimony on this point from our author.* "Some little effect, may, perhaps, be attributed to the direct action of the external conditions of life, and some little to habit; but he would be a bold man who would account by such agencies for the differences between a dray and a race horse, a greyhound and bloodhound, a carrier and tumbler pigeon. One of the most remarkable features in our domesticated races is that we see in them adaptation, not indeed to the animal's or plant's own good, but to man's use or fancy. Some variations useful to him have probably arisen suddenly, or by one step; many botanists, for instance, believe that the fuller's teazle, with its hooks, which cannot be rivalled by any mechanical contrivance, is only a variety of the wild dipsacus; and this amount of change may have suddenly risen in a seedling.— So it has probably been with the turnspit dog; and this is known to have been the case with the ancon sheep. But when we compare the dray horse and the race horse, the dromedary and camel, the various breeds of sheep fitted either for cultivated land or mountain pasture, with the wool of one breed good for one purpose, and that of another for another purpose; when we compare the many breeds of dogs, each good for man in

* Page 33.

very different ways; when we compare the game-cock, so pertinacious in battle, with other breeds so little quarrelsome, with "everlasting layers" which never desire to sit, and with the bantam so small and elegant; when we compare the host of agricultural, culinary, orchard, and flower garden races of plants, most useful to man at different seasons, and for different purposes, or so beautiful in his eyes, we must, I think, look further than to mere variability. We cannot suppose that all the breeds were suddenly produced as perfect and as useful as we now see them; indeed, in several cases, we know that this has not been their history. The key is man's power of accumulative selection: nature gives successive variations; man adds them up in certain directions useful to him. In this sense he may be said to make for himself useful breeds. The great power of this principle of selection is not hypothetical. It is certain that several of our eminent breeders have, within a single life-time, modified to a large extent, some breeds of cattle and sheep. In order fully to realize what they have done, it is necessary to read several of the many treatises devoted to this subject, and to inspect the animals. Breeders habitually speak of an animal's organization as something quite plastic which they can model almost as they please. If I had space, I could quote numerous passages to this effect from highly competent authorities. Youatt, who was probably better acquainted with the works of argriculturists than almost any other individual, and who was himself a very good judge of an animal, speaks of the principle of selection as "that which enables the agriculturist, not only to modify the character of his flock, but to change it altogether. It is the magician's wand, by which he may summon into life whatever form and mould he pleases. Lord Somerville, speaking of what breeders have done for sheep, says :—' it would seem as if they had chalked out upon a wall a form perfect in itself, and then had given it existence!' That most skilful breeder, Sir John Sebright, used to say, with respect to the pigeons, that ' he would produce any given feather in three years, but it would take him six years to obtain the head and beak.' In Saxony the importance of the principle of selection in regard to merino sheep is so fully recognised, that men follow it as a trade : the sheep are laid on a table and studied, like a picture by a connoisseur ; this is done three times at intervals of months, and the sheep are each time marked and classed, so that the very best may ultimately be selected for breeding. * * * The same principles are followed by the horticulturists; but the variations are here often more abrupt. No one supposes that our choicest productions have been produced by a single variation from the aboriginal stock. We have proofs that this is not so in some cases in which exact records have been kept ; thus to give a few trifling instances, the steadily increasing size of the common gooseberry may be quoted. We see an astonishing improvement in many florist's flowers, when the flowers of the present day are compared with drawings made twenty or thirty years ago. When a race of plants is pretty well established, the seed-raisers do not pick out the best plants, but merely go over the seed-beds and pull up the ' rogues,' as they call the plants that deviate from the proper standard. With animals this kind of selection is, in fact, also followed; for hardly any one is so careless as to allow his worst animals to breed."

That which man can do, through choosing the right agencies, towards the best development of plants and animals, that also, and infinitely more, can he accomplish for the benefit of his own species. Here, however, he must work chiefly through his intellectual and moral nature. As humanity is immeasurably above all else on the earth, so the means of securing its best good are worthy and exalted. We must, however, bear in mind that all human improvement, while it cares for the body, must demand imperatively for the perfection of the soul. To this end, all else, according to the laws of the Creator, must become subservient; and through these means will all superior mental and moral qualities become cultivated in ourselves, and be readily transmitted to our children.

"I think," continues Darwin, "there can be little doubt that use, in our domestic animals, strengthens and enlarges certain parts, and that disuse diminishes them, and that such modifications are inherited."

Here we have the whole secret of transmission. It is not the mere possession of remarkable faculties or qualities that will ensure their transmission, it is the exercise of them. Darwin gives many curious instances of the effects of use and disuse; amongst which are the wingless beetles of Madeira, and the blind animals of dark caves. Of the latter he says:

"It is well known that several animals of the most different classes which inhabit the caves of Styria and Kentucky, are blind. In some of the crabs, the footstalk for the eye remains, though the eye is gone; the stand for the telescope is there, though the telescope with its glasses has been lost. As it is difficult to imagine that eyes, though useless, could be in any way injurious to animals living in darkness, I attribute their loss wholly to disuse."

"Natural selection" has been gradually giving us gentler and more refined races of men. But culture here, as elsewhere, has stimulated every process. So would I quicken thought in this direction, would impress upon parents—especially upon the young, who may be parents in the future—that all the qualities of their being, even habits, tastes and tendencies, will be transmitted, with more or less modification, to their offspring.

It has been my aim in this article to call attention to the acknowledged fact of the transmission of faculties; and to suggest that by selecting our own standards of virtue in any direction we may not only go far towards attaining them for ourselves, but towards bequeathing them to posterity. As Nature co-works with man in his lowest grade of effort, so will she assist him in all higher departments. She who fosters, protects, and strengthens the plant and the animal, will never forget her crowning glory—man. Yet, just as she strengthens the strong, and allows the weak to be overcome and to perish in her irrational kingdom, so will it be in the rational, to a fearful extent.

CHAPTER TWENTY-SIXTH.

"PHILOSOPHICAL and Physiological Treatise on Natural Inheritance," is the title of a work recently published in Paris, by a well known physician, P. Lucas.

It is a book of great interest, containing fifteen hundred pages, illustrating its subject from a great variety of sources. This work treats especially of the transmission of the qualities of the mind producing the disposition to commit all manner of vices and crimes against society ; it is however more suitable for the medical profession, than for the popular reader.

After translating many pages on the transmitted tendency to robberies and murder, I discarded them as distasteful,—about as disagreeable, as so many pages from the " Newgate Calendar" would have been, but the following instances will illustrate sufficiently my position. " It is commonly supposed," says Giron de Buzareingue, that J. Rousseau is not preserved from error, that children are born without inclinations, and that one system of education would suit all ; it is however certain, that we are born with the propensities, as well as with temperament of those to whom we owe life, and it is often very difficult to say of an infant who can only scream and cry, whether its impatience or its anger proceeds from colic, from transmitted and innate character, or from its own habits. Nature is often taken for an effect of education, and rough measures are resorted to, in order to repress in a feeble being, propensities of ancient date, which form part of its organization. A child may be capricious and violent, because its father and mother are so."

"Does it not often happen," says Lavater, "that we find trait for trait in the son, the character, the temperament, and the greater part of the several qualities of the father, and how often does the character of the mother re-appear in her son, and that of the father in his daughter?"

A child may inherit from his father, or his mother, the most deplorable propensities.

He may inherit from them an inclination to drunkenness. Gall speaks of a Russian family, of which the father and grandfather, both perished prematurely, victims to their inclination for strong liquor: the grandson manifested from the age of five years, the most decided taste for the same liquors. Giron de Buzareingue, speaks of families where this unfortunate taste is transmitied by the mothers. We find in Louis himself, two examples which tend to support this form of inheritance, which he is so obstinate in combatting: the first is that of a family of Voitute, whose father and brother are passionately fond of good cheer and wine; whilst Voitute himself drinks nothing but water. The second is that of a family known personally to Louis; the head, and some of the children of this family, inherit from the father, gout with drunkenness. Louis denies transmission in these cases, on the sole plea, that *all* the children had not the same inclinations; this is but one error the more, in his paradox.

Drunkenness transmitted through families, may be allied to predispositions worse than even gout itself. Dr. Morean cites a case where this propensity is united in a young man, to insanity; the patient had no madmen in his family, but his father had the habit of intoxication; the son had not like him, abused the use of liquor, but every time that he was afflicted, he evinced a singular inclination to give himself up to it. A judicial journal relates a case still more deplorable. There were four brothers, all of them addicted to the most licentious drunkenness; the eldest of the family, threw himself into the water, and was drowned, the second hung himself, the third cut his throat with a razor, and the fourth threw himself from a third-story window, and only survived the injuries which this fall occasioned him, to be taken for excesses and violences, before the assizes.

The inheritance of an inclination to drunkenness, degenerated with them, into a mania for suicide.

"One of the pathological characteristics of drunkenness," says Professor Lucas, " is a certain degree of perversion, and a suspension of sense and intelligence. Drunkards see badly, do not perceive well, do not understand well, and comprehend no better than they understand or perceive. Children begotten in this state of mental stupidity and momentary obscurity of intelligence, are often born imbeciles, or complete idiots."*

* See Appendix J.

"However difficult it may be," says Hofland, "to collect facts in this regard, I shall nevertheless, be able to produce some examples of children engendered in drunkenness, who have remained idiots all their lives. According to Esquirol, an idiot named Brickton, was born of a mother, well educated, but her husband was an habitual drunkard. Some mothers of idiotic children have affirmed to Edward Sequin, that their husbands were in a decided state of drunkenness, at the moment of conception. A wife of Monistrol had three fine children; she suddenly abandoned herself to a frenzied passion for stimulants, and drunkenness became with her a confirmed habit; the children to whom she afterwards gave birth, were stunted, devoid of vigor, of disagreeable form, vacillating gait, torpid intelligence, of a low organization, and all of them died early. According to Rocch, if in conception, drunkenness joins its influence to that of the places where cretinism abounds, the children will not only be born idiots but cretins also."

These hereditary evils of drunkenness were evidently well understood by the ancients. The Greeks have translated this belief into allegory. The deformity of Vulcan, is by them attributed to the drunkenness of his father Jupiter, who indulged on one occasion too copiously in nectar. Diogenes said to a stupid youth, "Young man, thy father must have been very drunk, when thy mother conceived thee."

"Although," says Galen, "nature struggles against the effects of our vices, and our follies, yet the principal evils that attend upon a habit of drunkenness, are frequently t ansmitted from the parent to the child."* "The most common result exhibited by children procreated in this lamentable condition of the parents," says Hofaker, and Burbach, "is the almost entire absence of natural sensibility."*

The inheritance of insanity is of almost as ancient date as the disease itself. There is no writer on diseases, who has not observed it at the first glance cast upon that obscure and sad page of the history of human afflictions. Some voices that have protested against it, are lost in the crowd of those who proclaim

---

* Dr. Demeaux, who it seems has had special occasions for making the necessary observations, has lately communicated a most important paper, to the Academy, on the subject of drunkenness. According to his observations, running over a space of twelve years,—and he reports no case in which he has not had the formal and absolute declaration of the parents,—children conceived when one or both of the parents were in a state of drunkenness, are liable in a much larger proportion than others to epilepsy and idiocy. Of thirty-six epileptic persons, five (a large proportion) were absolutely conceived under this condition, while he reports several cases of idiocy, congenital paralysis, and other forms of cerebral disease, which he traces to the same origin. Dr. Demeaux demands of the profession, that attention should be turned to this subject; and he promises for a future occasion, a more detailed account of his own observations.—New York Daily Times.

* "Dr. Turner," principal of the Asylum for Inebriates in Binghamton, "has demonstrated that many inebriates and perhaps nearly all the class usually regarded as hopeless, are so from hereditary physical causes; that they must be treated as the subjects of disease, and can be reached only by hygienic means. * * * The hereditary nature of the disease of inebriety is shown by the statistics of insanity. Eighty per cent. of more than a thousand cases of delirium tremens which came under the observation of Dr. Turner, were the cases of children of intemperate parents."—North American Review, April, 1862.

it, and this melancholy truth in our day, finds but few skeptics.

There is no malady, says Foville, in which the action of transmission is better demonstrated, it is a point long since beyond question, and has taken its place amongst common notions. Illiterate witnesses are frequently heard to quote as an excuse for the acts of a culprit, and without being incited to it, the proofs of insanity, evinced by such and such a member of his family. Physicians in hospitals or asylums expressly devoted to the treatment of this malady, often find symptoms of insanity in the relations of the patient who place him there. There are but few exceptions where it does not attack the whole family. All the male descendants of a noble family in Hamburg, and from the time of the great-grandfather, remarkable for great military talents, were at the age of forty, stricken with insanity; there remained but one descendant, an officer like his ancestors, who was forbidden to marry by the senate of the city; the critical age arrived, he lost his reason. Three members of a family entered at one time the hospital for the insane in Philadelphia. In the asylum at Hartford has been seen a maniac, who was the eleventh of his family. A lady of whom Moran speaks, was the eighth; her father, two brothers, two sisters, two cousins and an aunt, were stricken like herself. Some two years since, the mental alienation of a whole family was seen in Brittany; father, mother, sisters, and brothers, whom the evil attacked like a contagion.

A lady of Cologne, young, robust, in good health, and at the time pregnant with her first child, saw a person fall at her feet in an epileptic fit; his convulsions and cries terrified her; some months later she was delivered, but it was not long before the child was attacked by epilepsy, and died at the end of a year.

The passion for gambling may be transmitted. A lady with whom I was acquainted, says the Chevalier Da Gamo Machado, enjoying a large fortune, had a passion for gambling, passing her nights at play; she died but little advanced in years of a pulmonary disease; her eldest son resembled her perfectly, being equally devoted to gambling, and passing his nights at the gaming table, like his mother, he died of consumption, and almost at the same age; his daughter inherited the same tastes, and died when still young.

CHAPTER TWENTY-SEVENTH.

It is often remarked, says Dr. Spurzheim, that certain mental faculties have the dominion in entire families. There is no order of talent where the celebrity of a family does not attest it. The art of oratory was so natural among the Hortensios, the Curios and the Selius, that it seemed to be transmitted from one to the other, and to be diffused even amongst the women. Hereditary political genius and eloquence are seen later in the Medici, and in the Pitt families.— Three women, all celebrated for their extraordinary intelligence in philosophy, and for the richest gifts of speech, Hypatia, Arete, and Madame de Stael, all had philosophers for fathers: the daughter of Neckar has almost caused her father to be forgotten. Mirabeau the father, was repeated in Mirabeau the Tribune. A more serious study of the " Friend of Man," shows in a strong light, what depth, originality and range of mind there was in this writer, whose singular genius was eclipsed in repeating itself, under a still more striking type, by that of his son. Another man, whose name shines with a celebrity as strange in a different way, was Michael Nostradamus, that popular prophet of the sixteenth century, Doctor and Professor of Medicine at Montpelier—a man truly extraordinary, and to whose science his adversaries themselves have rendered justice; he gloried in being descended from a tribe renowned for the gift of prophecy. His paternal and maternal grandparents were celebrated physicians; his son Cæsar was at once a good poet, an excellent painter, and an able historian.

Antiquity counts no less than eight tragic poets in the family of Eschylus. The same kind of talent is remarked in the family of Tasso; Bernardo Tasso, the father of Torquato, possessed the gift of poetry, of which his son had the genius. The poetry of Racine lived again, without doubt less fruitful and less inspired, but still recognizable, in the verses of his son.

Facts of inheritance abound in sculpture, painting, and the musical art. The illustrious German Pilon, whose name has been given to one of the fine galleries at the Louvre, which bear the name of the French sculptors, was the son of a very distinguished sculptor of Mentz. It was in the studio of his father that he imbibed the elements of the art. John Flaxman, a celebrated English sculptor, the author of the most remarkable bas-reliefs of Covent Garden theatre, and of several monuments at Chichester and Westminster, was the son of a modeler of figures in plaster. The rival of Canova, Albert Thorswalden, who was stricken by death in his native city in the midst of his glory, was the son of a poor sculptor, Gotschalk Thorswalden.

Among painters, we see the father of Raphael, himself a painter. The mother of Van Dyke had a remark able talent for painting flowers. Le Parmegiano lost his father when still young, but his uncles were painters. Van Loo was the brother, the grandson, and the great-grandson of painters. The two younger brothers of Titian, his son, his nephew and grandnephew, were alike painters. Horace Vernet is the son of Charles Vernet, of such rare talent in painting horses; and he is the grandson of that Joseph Vernet so celebrated for his marine views; his brother, although a bookseller, had a true passion for painting, and it is said that there are paintings of his which have been taken for those of his brother.

The same succession of musical genius is remarked in families: the father of Mozart was a violinist of reputation, and the sister of the illustrious composer had, like her brother, displayed the most precocious talent for music. He left two sons; one of them is director of music at Lemburg. Beethoven was the son of a tenor: quite a crowd of composers have appeared in the family of John Sebastian Bach, a man of high musical celebrity.

The influence of the father over all the elements and all the forms of the mental faculties, is very decided: elevation of mind, vigor of intelligence, eloquence, poetry, music, sculpture, painting, every kind of tendency and every type of talent may in some manner radiate from his mind into those of his children. To the preceding examples which we hav given, we will add those of Dr. Johnson and Burns.

The father of Dr. Johnson, says his enthusiastic biographer, Boswell, was a tall and robust man: he had a great compass of intelligence, and a very powerful activity of mind; nevertheless, as in the hardest rock corrupt veins are found, he had in him a tinge of that evil whose nature escapes the most minute investigation, although its effects may be but too well known to make it the torment of life. It manifested itself in him in a profound distaste for all the pursuits which move the greater part of humanity, and his mind was wholly under the dominion of an incessant melancholy: under a more sombre and original form Johnson inherited this melancholy, and in him it was almost transformed into insanity. He was crazy all his life, without being any the less wise. The mother of Johnson was a woman of superior intelligence, and it is said of her that well as she certainly knew his merit she had too much sense to be vain of him.

Burns, who had, like Dr. Johnson, a decided inclination to melancholy and a hypochondriacal temperament, also owed to his father the force, and at the same time the physical and moral irritability of his organization. In features and address he bore a strange resemblance to his mother; it is from her he inherited the passion for ballads and popular songs—germs of his future greatness as a poet.

The biographies of the most celebrated men abound with similar facts, but daily observations are as instructive on this point, and the proofs of the inheritance of intellectual disorders are so decisive that they do not admit of the slightest doubt. There is no family where the intellectual type of the father is not repeated in different degrees in the children.

History, says Girou, furnishes an infinity of examples of the moral resemblance of the father to the daughter, and of the mother to the son. Amongst orators and political men, Cleobulus of Rhodes, Antipater, Selius, Hortentius, Cicero, Cato; among kings and emperors, Caligula, Charlemagne, Alphonso IX., of Castile, Philip I., Louis XII., Henry II., of Valois, John II., of Navarre, Henry VIII., of England, Henry IV., Gustavus Adolphus, &c., are repeated in their daughters. Olympias, Cratesopolis, Cornelia, Livia, Faustina, Loemia, Fredegonde, Margaret of Brabant, Charlotte of Savoie, Berengaria, Blanche, Urruca, Catherine de Medici, Marie de Medici, Anne of Austria, and the wife of Cromwell, in her son. We might add to to the latter the mother of the two Chéniers, of Goëthe, Walter Scott, Napoleon, and perhaps that of the King of Rome. Is it not singular to find in the greater part of the women who amongst the ancients have shone for intelligence and philosophy, so many living echoes and softened rays of the genius of their fathers? It was unto Myia, Arignote, and Damo, his daughters, that the soul of Pythagoras passed. The first enjoyed a great celebrity; the writings of the second still existed at the time of Porphyrus; and it was to Damo that Pythagoras entrusted all his writings. Hypatia, whose knowledge and genius awoke at once the admiration, the love, and the jealousy of men, was the daughter of Theon, a famous philosopher, geometrician and mathematician of Alexandria.

The principal portion of Professor Lucas's book is devoted to the consideration of inherited tendencies to physical disease, and all its concomitant evils. We will, in the next chapter, endeavor to show the value and the importance of high health, both for ourselves and for our children. To many, it may appear a work of supererogation, while others will accept thankfully the thoughts of the best writers of the age on the subject.

CHAPTER TWENTY-EIGHTH.

"Without health, an actual blight rests on the powers both of body and mind. Such is the intimate connection between them, that if the one is disturbed, the influence is reflected on the other. Sound thinking is dependent upon the soundness of the body. The brain, the medium through which the soul of man receives its impressions from without, and eliminates its thoughts from within, is a material part of this body. From this great nervous centre are poured forth the vital streams of health. There, no doubt, are first made the impressions, which disturb, derange, and direct the healthy action."[*]

"Health," says Carlyle, "is a great matter both to the possessor of it, and to others. On the whole, that humorist in the moral essays, was not so far out, who determined on honoring health only; and so instead of humbling himself to the highborn, to the rich and well dressed, insisted on doffing his hat to the healthy: coronetted carriages with pale faces in them, passed by as failures, miserable and lamentable, trucks with

[*] Dr. Bayard.

ruddy cheeked health dragging at them were greeted as successful and venerable; for does not health mean harmony, the synonym of all that is true, justly ordered good; is it not in some sense the net total, as shown by experience, of whatever truth is in us? The healthy man is a most meritorious product of nature, as far at he goes. A healthy baby is good; but a soul in right health,—it is the thing beyond all others to be prayed for; the blessedest thing that earth receives of Heaven. * * * The healthy soul discovers what is good and adheres to it, and retains it, discerns what is bad, and spontaneously casts it off. An instinct from Nature herself, like that which guides wild animals of the forest to their food, shows him what he shall do, and what he shall abstain from. The false and the foreign will not adhere to him; cant and all fantastic diseased incrustations are impossible. This thing canst thou work with and profit by, this thing is substantial and worthy; that other thing, thou canst not work with, it is trivial and inapt; so speaks unerringly the inward monition of man's whole nature. * * * * Blessed is the healthy nature, it is the coherent, sweetly coöperative, not incoherent, self-distracting, self-destructive one! In the harmonious adjustment and play of all the faculties, the just balance of one's self, gives a just feeling towards all men and all things. Glad light from within radiates outwards, and enlightens and embellishes."

"The physical evils of commercial life," Thrakrah says, "would be considerably reduced if men reflected that the sucess of business may be prevented by the very means used to promote it. Excessive application and anxiety, by disordering the animal economy, weaken the mental powers. Our opinions are affected by the states of the body, and our judgment often perverted. If a clear head be required in commercial transactions, a healthy state of the body is of the first importance, a healthy body is incompatible with excessive application of mind—with the want of exercise and fresh air."

A strong mind can never work well in a weak body. Its efforts must be fitful and capricious, probably unhealthy. "Intellect," says the Rev. D. A. Wasson, "in a weak body, is like gold in the pocket of a spen swimmer, the richer he would be, under other circumstances, by so much the more is his danger now." The mind has a powerful sovereignty over the body; it can nerve it to a most superhuman effort, when occasion requires; but this power is only transient,—the frail body will be broken by the force within—exhausted by the ceaseless activity,—and fretted away by the restless chafing of the strong spirit.

Healthy men with great muscular frames and hardy good sense, but illiterate and undisciplined in mind, have been better workers in the world than our sickly scholars. "It is true," says Dr. A. G. Howe, "that the real nobles, the class of veritable leaders of mankind, has to be recruited every now and then by descending into the great bosom of the people, and fetching up from thence, fresh spirits full of native energy, to supply its own exhaustion; and it rises from every fall to the earth, Antæus-like, fresher and stronger than ever. But it will always be seen that the mighty men who rise up from among the laboring class are not born of parents who were over-worked, and that they have not been over-worked themselves; that circumstances have favored the exercise of a brain and a nervous system which were naturally vigorous, and that often they have preserved the happy mean of moderate exercise of mind and body." In this country where intellectual life is free to all, this is the rule. Yet generations of culture are of incalculable importance. How much will be achieved then, when the whole being is developed and strengthened in harmony?

"All through the life of a pure-minded, but feeble bodied man," says Horace Man, "his path is lined with Memory's gravestones, which mark the spots where noble enterprises perished for lack of physical vigor to embody them into deeds." Poor Horace Man is himself an illustration of his own statement. He died in the prime of life, because his physical system was not strong enough to keep pace with the mental. It succumbed in the effort; and his own last great enterprise, the upbuilding of a noble institution of learning for the sons and daughters of the people, was left to struggle with difficulties in the very infancy of its existence.

There is no other civilized nation which is so regardless of health as our own; probably no other so indifferent to exercise, to food, to recreations that will strengthen, protect and invigorate the system. Until lately, athletic sports and games were quite out of fashion here. Whilst the Frenchman danced, and the Englishman rode horseback, the American gentleman crossed his legs and dozed in his easy chair, dreaming of cash accounts, whether asleep or awake. While the English woman would take her constitutional walk of five or ten miles for her health's sake, the American would take an airing in her carriage, and make calls for fashion's sake. Little wonder that we have become, par eminence, the nation that "enjoys poor health"! But " muscle is looking up " in democratic America as well as elsewhere. The evidences of this are not only to be found in our " Benicia Boy," " Champion of the World ;" but in our gymnasiums, yacht races, pedestrian excursions, skating parties, and above all, in the sledding and hoop rolling of our juveniles of both sexes; and also in the multiplication of country residences, country life, and intelligent gentleman farmers. Vigorous habits may hereafter be tolerated, and good health may finally become respectable, not necessarily attaching to itself the suspicion of coarseness or vulgarity.

Rev. T. W. Higginson says, " Our American saintship, also, is beginning to have a body to it, a 'Body of Divinity,' indeed. Look at our three great popular preachers. The vigor of the paternal blacksmith still swings the sinewy arm of Beecher ; Parker performed the labor, mental and physical, of four able-bodied men, until even his great strength yielded ; and if ever dyspepsia attacks the burly frame of Chapin, we fancy that dyspepsia will get the worst of it."

In this age of progress we have also the " Movement Cure," imported, it is true, but rapidly becoming acclimated. There is but one step between cure and prevention, and we are taking that also. One may see clearly that Movement Prevention is yet destined to become fashionable, especially among ladies of high culture. Fashion already has a laurel wreath for our skaters. She has decided it is better our girls should skate races with their brothers and win, than to vie with them in effeminacy, and probably fail, as they must, while men are born of effeminate mothers.

I have heard of one father who defied fashion for his daughter's sake. This was years ago, and how much this one example may have done towards changing popular tastes, it would be a pleasant thing to determine. "Harriet Hosmer," says Mrs. Ellet, "is the only surviving daughter of a physician, who, having lost wife and child by consumption, and fearing a like fate for the survivor, gave her horse, dog, gun and boat, and insisted upon an out-door life as indispensible to health. A fearless horsewoman, a good shot, adept in rowing, swimming, diving, skating, Harriet Hosmer is a singular instance of what judicious training will effect in conquering even hereditary taint of constitution.

"Willingly as the active, energetic child acquiesced in her father's wishes, she contrived, at the same time, to gratify and develope her own peculiar tastes; and many a time and oft, when the worthy doctor may have flattered himself that his darling was in active exercise, she might have been found in a certain clay-pit not very far from the paternal residence making early attempts at modeling horses, dogs, sheep, men and women, and any object which attracted her attention.' It has been well said, that the "triumphs of Rosa Bonheur and Harriet Hosmer grew out of a free and vigorous training, and they learned to develope muscle by using it."

So the great ones of earth have defied the shallow customs which would have fettered them; and in doing this, they found room for the unfolding of greatness. No parlor-nursed child could have become a Bonheur or a Hosmer.

It is not so germain to our subject to treat of education or habits subsequent to birth, as to indicate the effects of habits and constitutional tendencies in the parents upon the child yet unborn. Yet they are twin topics, almost inseparable, and equally important.

CHAPTER TWENTY-NINTH.

I HAVE very little to suggest concerning the ordinary routine of study to which American children are subjected. Popular attention is already strongly enlisted in that direction; yet I cannot refrain from a brief chapter upon the every-day unconscious influences which are the great and permanent moulders of the character in every age. The theme is exhaustless; but each needs to be stimulated in this direction, not merely for the benefit of the rising generation, but for his own good also, as our education is never finished—at least "on this side of the cloud."

Any suggestion which arouses the attention is itself a most powerful educator. It impresses itself upon the mind in colors more or less enduring, where it remains a fixed influence, which is never afterwards wholly destroyed.

Mrs. Glass' famous receipt for cooking a hare begins, "First catch your hare." First give us the right organization, or we cannot develope the right character.*

---

* The truth of this remark is illustrated by the well-known fact that at every examination of the cadets at West Point one-third of the number are rejected as mentally or physically unqualified to pass the severe examination to which they are subjected.

That children should be well-born is the first and the greatest consideration; but one, it would seem, which produces the least influence upon mankind. In some instances, it looks indeed " as though Nature's journeymen had made men, and not made them well, they imitated humanity so abominably."

It is wise to think largely of the ample wealth of old patrician blood, of the many virtues of a spotless lineage, inherited from a brave and noble ancestry of many generations. Yet if these born noblemen were educated plebeians, they would soon fall into the vulgar ranks, like the finest garden flower when it is cast out to the neglect and dust of the wayside. There is a social atmosphere in which each one lives and breathes from his childhood up, which nourishes his growing character as the food he takes nourishes and builds up his physical system.

The steadily refining influence of an elevated social life, will leave its deposit of fine gold upon the commonest nature; and the endless platitudes of silly and weak people will leave a strata of earthiness upon the brightest genius, if it be hampered by their companionship. It is useless to fancy ourselves exceptions to this general rule; for we all have more or less of the chameleon in our natures, and reflect the color of the light which shines upon us from an innate necessity. How else shall we account for the moral epidemics which from time to time overspread every country.

If there are a few prophets who can see far beyond the times and are able to utter oracles for future ages, it is because they do not live in the present and feel its influences; they live apart, in a world of their own—the Past; from whom they can trace human progress from the remotest ages; and from what has been, are able to infer what will be: hence their faith in the future, which sometimes appears inspiration.— Not so, the people; they are educated by their associates and their surroundings. It would be as absurd to ridicule the flowers for blooming in the spring, or the trees for dropping their leaves in the winter, as to jeer at the popular tendencies of our fellow beings.— Our true wisdom consists in recognising and directing the social impetus which springs up so readily on all occasions—which becomes an enthusiasm in moments of excitement—a quiet sentiment in hours of calmness, and which, surrounding us like an atmosphere, everywhere and at all times, is denominated the spirit of the age.

It would be as impossible for the nineteenth century to enter into the opinions and sentiments of the middle ages, as for Boston and Charleston to arrive at the same social conclusions upon any question of moment. Yet it is the people, ourselves and our neighbors, who make this social power, which reacts again upon us all. This class of influences, although most powerful, are frequently more local than general. Almost every community has its own modifying causes which mould public opinion in that locality, until each class, clique and circle has its own views, sentiments and tendencies, inherited from the past, or imbibed from the peculiar influences to which they are subjected. Each family has its type of character; but who shall say whether it be not as much modified by its circumstances—by the family beliefs and feelings, as by its inherited proclivities. I have known one child of a family to be adopted elsewhere and brought up under entirely different circumstances, to differ from all his kindred in looks, thoughts, style of manners, and character.* Again and again have such examples been repeated with more or less marked effect, until it cannot be doubted that education is at least the powerful rival and competitor of inherited tendencies in moulding the character of mankind. Every object in nature is many-sided; the grass-blade is double-edged; the leaf has its two faces, and the crystal its several planes. So every social and moral question has its many stand-points for discussion.

If we would truly improve the race, we must be constant in our appliances, not only before birth, but until death. That effects follow causes is a principle which can never be too thoroughly interwoven with all practical life. I am especially desirous to impress the mind with the almost omnipotence of the unconscious and undesigned, but ever ceaseless influences which round and finish all characters. Influences, direct and intentional, may be brought to bear with ample force; but they are often wholly or partially counteracted by gentle and unrecognized causes, each touching lightly, here a little, and there a little, unseen and unfelt, but with a finger as resistless as fate itself.

As a nation, we are careful to give our youth school

---

* Children who have inherited active animal propensities, accompanied by a weak will, or any peculiar family idiosyncracies, are, of course, exceptions to this general rule.

knowledge. In this sense, no community was ever better educated. But our children mingle more freely and sooner with the world, and are earlier matured mentally than any other people; and thus while they are taught one thing by precept, they can learn quite another by example. We give the little girl a moral lesson against vanity; but, at the same time, we place her under circumstances where she finds that display is the first consideration: of course she is moulded by the strongest influence. We would teach a son to be wise, honest, and diligent, but we allow him to associate with the weak, idle and unprincipled; if he becomes a fop or a black-leg we must blame ourselves, rather than the pliant youth. A week of precept is worth less than an hour of example; just as seven sermons would produce less impression than one attractive moral story.

Our children may be ever so well born, but unless we learn the potent secret of strongly and rightly enlisting them in any direction which we may desire, they never can be well trained.

Every passion and emotion of the human heart, whether good or evil, has a magnetic power which will attract, more or less, each person who comes within its charmed circle. So a genuine enthusiasm, whatever its moral tone, is contagious; but the boy of five and the lad of sixteen will take it more certainly than the man of fixed principles. It is absolutely impossible to associate intimately with any one who has decided tastes and interests in any direction, and who is frank in the expression of his sympathies, without feeling yourself drawn towards him into some degree of appreciation. You catch his spirit, you find your own views widening to take in his, you realize that there is more in life than you had thought, and there comes a new sense of expansiveness to your own powers. Here is the great advantage of mingling freely with a frank diversity of minds. The traveler, if he has the skill to look below the surface of things, returns a much wiser man. Foreign nations give him foreign thoughts, which, when harmonized with his own, the old thought range is vastly widened. But one's associations need to be close, easy, and familiar if he would penetrate to the sources of another's strength and power in any direction. Literary and social clubs, scientific and philanthropic societies, churches, all these knit closely the bonds of association. They mingle heads and hearts till each takes to himself something from the lives of all. Isolation is dwarfing in its tendencies, association is the continued opening-up of wider experiences. The man of letters finds his companionship with his authors; the naturalist may find his in the facts and laws he is studying; but there is nothing like the loving thoughts and sympathies of a friend to quicken sympathies in another.

What the parents love and do, the children will love and do also; they catch the spirit of it by inspiration. If people would remember this, in educating their children, a far less number would disappoint the hopes of parents. "Don't you know," quoth little Ben in his sweet voice, "that an idiot is a person who doesn't know an arbor vitæ from a pine; he don't know anything?" "The young human scion," says Mr. Higginson, " knew the flowers by name before he knew his letters, and used their symbols more readily." It was doubtless the knowedge and the steady fervent love of those about him, for natural objects, which made him as familiar with trees, as with his games and playthings. No dry, formal teaching could have secured this object; for every young person is influenced more by the likes and dislikes of those about him, than by their precepts. Do you desire to give your son gentlemanly manners? Don't bore him with injunctions, but give him gentlemanly associates. Do you wish to give him a correct and fluent use of the noble English language? Don't send him to a school where the teacher and pupils speak only in provincialisms. Do you wish your son to cultivate any art or science? Place him with people who are in love with those things.

"The child is father to the man." That which is good for your children is equally good for yourself. Any one of fair abilities can become about what he pleases, in culture, and in character; but, in order to do this, he must make use of the right means. He must agree with Carlyle that " many a bright genius is smothered under a too vigorous digestion,"—must eschew self-indulgence and love of ease,—must live in accordance with the laws of life and health ; and must conscientiously believe with Bacon, " that all knowedge is his province."

If the education of youth could have a more practical bent, and be carried on as an every day and every hour matter, the world would assume a new character in a single generation. The good effect would be more immediate and more apparent, than that resulting from any amount of attention bestowed for the ante-natal development of the race. Yet the two are related to each other, as the foundation to the superstructure. A showy, pretentious building, erected on the sands, has scriptural authority for its unsoundness and instability. So a good basis if it be not worthily crowned with a fitting education, is of little worth.

Eternal vigilance is the price of all noblest good for ourselves and for our children. Every work which seeks the broadest development of .the race, must look for its needs not only in the present, but in the light of the past of all nations and ages. By thus enlarging its ends and aims, it best comprehends the most sacred interests of humanity; and every reflecting mind will become impressed with the necessity and importance of a more perfect development of the race.

THE MOTHER'S PRAYER.

I HAVE the great satisfaction to be able to enrich this volume with the following prayer, contributed by one of our divines well known to the public by his services in the cause of humanity and right. I recommend it to the attenon of every expectant mother, as a supplication to DIVINE GOODNESS for the most valuable gift which it is possible to receive in this world, not only for herself, but for the generations of all time.

PRAYER.

O GOD! my Creator! Thou that didst cover me in my mother's womb, and in whose book all my members were written, which in continuance were fashioned when as yet there was none of them. Hear the humble prayer of thy handmaid, in whom Thou hast planted the hope of offspring! Thou alone knowest what is the way of the Spirit; and how the bones do grow in the womb of her that is with child. Thy servant bows in adoration of the mystery by which Thou kindlest the living soul from the dust and ashes of mortal flesh. Framer of our bodies and Father of our spirits!—mercifully regard thine handmaid while she carries this germ of an immortal being in her loins! Help her to control every carnal appetite or mental passion that might injure the precious trust committed unto her! May meek and holy thoughts prevail in her heart, while this babe is hid beneath it; so that her sins and caprices may not be communicated to her seed, but rather Thy Holy Spirit, and the mind of Christ, Thy Holy Child. In the name of Him who bore the Cross, make Thy servant patient under any weariness or sorrow belonging to her condition! Against the hour of her labor, enable her to strengthen her heart with thoughts of the joy she shall feel, when her child shall see the light and breathe the breath of life! Make the holy thing which is to come out of her, a joy to its parents, a benefit to the world, and an heir of salvation. And to that end, render her, whose reins Thou hast possessed, more calm in trust, purer in thought, more constant in obedience, and closer in her walk with Thee—until it shall please Thee to complete the full time of her delivery, and to lay this unborn child in thy handmaid's bosom! Hear, O Father, for the sake of Thy dear Son, our Lord and Saviour Jesus Christ. *Amen.*

APPENDIX.

APPENDIX A.

The following extract is from "Physiology of Common Life," by Lewes. "The Qualities we inherit from our Parents," page 314, vol. 2.

"'That boy is the very image of his mother'! is the exclamation frequently heard; and not less frequently, 'That boy is remarkably unlike his parents'! We also hear it said, 'He has his father's talent, or his mother's sharpness,' and conversely, 'He has none of the family talent.' That the sons of remarkable men are generally dunces, and that men of genius have remarkable mothers, are two very questionable statements which have become proverbial.

"Such contradictory statements seem to indicate that qualities are and are not inherited from parents; that inheritance is very much a matter of chance, and that what we usually suppose to be evidence of hereditary transmission, is really nothing more than coincidence. This seems to be the view taken by Mr. Buckle; in his remarkable work there is the following passage, which must excite the physiologist's astonishment: " We often hear of hereditary talents, hereditary vices, and hereditary virtues; but whoever will critically examine the evidence, will find that we have no proof of their existence. The way in which they are commonly proved is in the highest degree illogical, the usual course being for writers to collect instances of some mental peculiarity found in the parent and in his child, and then to infer that the peculiarity was bequeathed. By this mode of reasoning we might demonstrate any proposition, since in any large field of inquiry there are a sufficient number of empirical coincidences to make a plausible case in favor of whatever view a man chooses to advocate."*

It must be admitted that many of the cases collected to prove hereditary transmission have been allowed to pass unchallenged by criticism, and many of them are worthless as evidence, but is Mr. Buckle prepared to deny that the tendencies and peculiarities of men depend on their organizations? If he is not prepared to deny this, his criticism is illogical, since there can be no shadow of doubt that organisms are inherited. He will not say that it is a mere coincidence which preserves intact the various "breeds" of animals; which makes the bull-dog and the terrier; which makes the Jews all over the world resemble Jews, because they keep their race free from admixture, by never marrying into other races; which gives us short-horned cattle and fan-tailed pigeons; and which makes the pedigree of a horse or dog, a value estimated in hard cash. Unless parents transmitted to offspring their organizations, their peculiarities and excellencies, there would be no such thing as a breed or a race. The cur would run the same chance as the best bred dog of turning out valuable. The grey-hound might point, and the cart-horse win the Derby. Daily experience tells us that this is impossible. Science tells us that there is no such thing as chance. Physiology tells us

* Buckle: Civilization in England, I., 61.

that the offspring always, and necessarily, inherits its organization from the parents; and if the organization is inherited, then with it must be inherited its tendencies and aptitudes. Mr. Buckle seems to have been misled by that which conceals the fact of transmission from ordinary apprehension, namely, the very great number of instances in which the offspring does not resemble either parent; or rather in which the resemblance is not *discernable* by us. If the law of transmission is not a figment, these seeming contradictions are susceptible of explanation; and in the course of the brief survey which will here be given, I hope to be able to convince the reader that an explanation is possible.

We must first note the indubitable fact that the organization of the offspring always and necessarily resembles that of the parents in its *general* character. So uniform is our experience of this constancy, that nothing would be more incredible than that negro parents should give birth to a child with the straight hair, aquiline nose, small heels, &c., of a European; or that two sheep should produce a goat. But while there is this constancy in the transmission of *general* characters, there is considerable variation in the transmission of individual peculiarities. One of the negro parents may be tall, robust, joyous, stupid; the other, short, feeble, querulous, clever; now as the child cannot be at once short and tall, clever and stupid, feeble and robust, in inheriting its parents' organizations it may resemble one of the parents more than the other, or may apparently resemble neither, by being a mingling of the two. It is the fact of double parentage, and double inheritance, with an inequality in the amount of influence exercised by each parent, which complicates the question, and produces the seeming contradictions to the law of transmission. Let two Jews produce offspring, and inasmuch as both parents have the Jewish physiognomy, the offspring will be unmistakably Jewish;

but let the Jew and the Saxon produce offspring, and the mingling of these two different organizations will be as visible in the offspring as it is in the mulatto, or in any other cross breed.

People often express surprise at observing the strange differences in aspect and disposition between brothers bred up together in the same nursery, and under similar influencies. From Cain and Abel, to the brothers Bonaparte, the diversity in families has been a standing marvel. Nay, such diversities are observed not only between brothers, but between twins; and it was noticed in the striking case of the celebrated Rita and Christina, twins who were so *fused together* that they had only one body and one pair of legs between them, with two heads and four arms, yet they manifested very different dispositions and tempers.* The same was observed of the Presburg twins, the Siamese twins, and of the African twins, recently exhibited in London. The cause of these diversities is the inequality with which the parental organizations were inherited; both parents contributing their elements, but these elements were differently compounded.

It is to this inequality in the influence of a particular parent that we must attribute the fact, that, while certain peculiarities, trifling and even whimsical, are sometimes seen to be transmitted, they are not uniformly transmitted. * * * The truth of the matter seems to be this: The organization of the parent is transmitted, and with that organization, all those characters and tendencies which the organization in activity would naturally manifest. A habit, or a trick, which has been acquired, and so long established that it may be said to be *organized* in the individual—whose mechanism has *grown* to its performance—will stand the

* Geoffroy St. Hilaire: Philosophic Anatomique, 11.

same chance of being inherited, as the bulk of bone and muscle, or the sensibility of the nervous system. An idiosyncracy which results from some organic disposition—say for example, the repugnance to animal food—may as easily be inherited as a good constitution, or a scrofulous tendency. Explain it as we may, there is no fact more certain than that a habit once firmly fixed, once "organized" in the individual, becomes almost as susceptible of transmission as any normal tendency. Pointer pups inherit the aptitude, *i. e.* the organization fitting them for easily learning to "point;" and this aptitude is sometimes so strong that they will point before they have been taught. It is the same with dogs that have been taught to "beg." I had a pup, taken from its mother at six weeks old, and before, therefore, it could have learned to beg from her, which spontaneously took to begging for everything it wanted; and one day I found it opposite a rabbit hutch, begging apparently, the rabbits to come and play. Girou relates that he knew a man who had the habit of sleeping on his back, with his right leg crossed over his left. One of his daughters showed the same peculiarity from her birth upwards, and constantly assumed the same attitude in her cradle. Venette knew a woman who, without being lame, had a sort of limp in her right leg; her daughter had the same defect in her right leg. Every one's experience will furnish examples of trifling peculiarities of manner—too individual to be mistaken—which are manifested by children who have never seen the parents they imitate. Nor is there anything surprising in this. The habit or manner, the attitude or trick, results from some peculiarity in the bodily framework, congenital or acquired, and this peculiarity is transmitted in the framework. It would *always* be transmitted were there not the counter-influence of a second parent, whose organization is also inherited. This second parent has not the peculiarity, and the peculiarity may therefore be counteracted by her influence. Two pointers will produce pups that easily learn to point, or even do so spontaneously; but if a pointer be crossed with a setter, it is very likely some of the pups will not point at all, although some may inherit the parental tendency. If a man with a great musical aptitude marry a woman with none, it is probable that of two children one will inherit the musical aptitude, and the other be as insensible as the mother; but it is also probable that both will inherit the aptitude, or that neither will. Whenever we observe vigorous constancy in the transmission of qualities—as in the breeds of animals—the secret is that both parents had more or less of these qualities. Whenever we observe inconstancy in the transmission, the secret is, that only one parent had the qualities; and inasmuch as both parents transmit their organizations, the double influence determines the product.

Instead, therefore, of feeling any surprise at a quality not being inherited when only one parent had that quality, we must anticipate such a result being very frequent; and our attention should rather be fixed on the numerous cases in which the quality is transmitted in spite of the influence of the other parent. Two consumptive parents will inevitably bring forth consumptive or scrofulous children; but one consumptive and one vigorous parent will bring forth children, none of which may be consumptive or scrofulous, or only some of them, or *all* of them. These variations throw no doubt of inheritance, but are in strict conformity with it; because no sooner are disturbing influences removed than the law acts with unvarying uniformity. * * * Tendencies to particular vices are inherited, and are exhibited in cases where the early death of the parents, or the removal of the children in infancy, prevents the idea of any imitation or effect of education being the cause. That the organization of a thief is transmitted from father to son through generations, seems tolerably certain. Gall has cited some striking examples. And murder, like talent, seems occasionalty to run in families.

Mr. Lewes gives many remarkable instances of the hereditary transmission of insanity, of blindness, of the various nervous diseases, and of longevity. The theory generally adopted by physiologists, that the male parent gives the external or locomotive organs, and the female the internal or vital organs, is thus opposed by this author. "Moreover, if the theory we are combating be admitted—if the father bestows the nervous system—how are we to explain the notorious inferiority of the children of great men? There is considerable exaggeration afloat on this matter, and able men have been called nullities because they have not manifested the great talents of their fathers; but allowing for all over-statement, the palpable fact of the inferiority of some sons to their fathers is beyond dispute, and has helped to foster the idea of all great men owing their genius to their mothers, an idea which will not bear confrontation with facts. Many men of genius have had remarkable mothers; and that one such instance could be cited is sufficient to prove the error both of the hypothesis which refers the nervous system to paternal influence, and of the hypothesis which only refers the preponderance to the paternal influence. If the male preponderates, how is it that Pericles, who 'carried the weapons of Zeus upon his tongue,' produced nothing better than a Paralus and a Xanthippus? How came the infamous Lysimachus from the austere Aristides? How was the weighty intellect of Thucydides left to be represented by an idiotic Milesius, and a stupid Stephanus? Where was the great soul of Oliver Cromwell in his son Richard? Who were the inheritors of Henry 1V.

and Peter the Great? What were Shakespeare's children, and Milton's daughters? What was Addison's only son? an idiot. Unless the mother preponderated in these and similar instances, we are without an explanation; for it being proved as a law of heritage, that the individual does transmit his qualities to his offspring, it is only on the supposition of both individuals transmitting their organizations, and the one modifying the other, that such anomalies are conceivable. When the paternal influence is not counteracted, we see it transmitted. Hence the common remark, 'talent runs in families.' The proverbial phrases, 'L'esprit des Mortemarts,' and the 'wit of the Sheridans,' imply this transmission from father to son. Bernardo Tasso was a considerable poet, and his son Torquato inherited his faculties, hightened by the influence of the mother. The two Herschels, the two Colemans, the Kemble family, and the Coleridges, will at once occur to the reader; but the most striking example known to us is that of the family which boasted Jean Sebastian Bach as the culminating illustration of a musical genius, which more or less was distributed over three hundred Bachs, the children of very various mothers.

" Here a skeptical reader may be tempted to ask, how a man of genius is ever produced if the child is the repetition of his parents? How can two parents of ordinary capacity produce a child of extraordinary power? The answer must be postponed until we come to treat of secondary influences. For the present we content ourselves with insisting on the conclusions to which the foregoing survey of facts has led, namely, that *both* parents are *always* represented in the offspring; and although the male influence is sometimes seen to preponderate in one direction, and the female influence in another, yet this direction is by no means constant, is often reversed, and admits of no absolute reduction to a known formula. * * * It is now time that we should direct our attention to some of the perturbing causes which mask the laws of transmission from our perfect apprehension. While proclaiming as absolute the law of individual transmission, while proclaiming that the parents are always reproduced in the offspring, we are met by the obvious fact of the offspring often exhibiting so marked a departure from their parents, being so different in form and disposition, that the law seems at fault. We may point to the fact of a genius suddenly starting up in an ordinary family, or to a thousand illustrative examples in which the law of transmission seems at fault. To explain these would be to have mastered the whole mystery of heritage; all that we can do is to mention some of the known perturbing influences." For these, we must refer the reader to Mr. Lewes's book, p. 338, second volume.

The following extract coroborates the preceding views.*

"Hereditary transmission, displayed alike in all the plants we cultivate, in all the animals we breed, and in the human race, applies not only to physical, but to psychical peculiarities. It is not simply that a modified form of constitution produced by new habits of life, is bequeathed to future generations, but it is that the modified nervous tendencies produced by such new habits of life, are also bequeathed : and if the new habits of life become permanent, the tendencies become permanent. This is illustrated in every creature respecting which we have the requisite experience, from man downwards. Though among the families of civilized society, the change of occupation and habits from generation to generation, and the intermarriage of families having different occupations and habits, very greatly confuse the evidence

---

* Spencer's Principles of Psychology, p. 526.

of psychical transmission, yet it needs but to consider national characters in which these disturbing causes are averaged, to see distinctly that mental peculiarities produced by habit become hereditary. We know that they are warlike, peaceful, nomadic, maritime, hunting, commercial races — races independent or slavish, active or slothful, — races that display great varieties of disposition; we know that many of these, if not all, have a common origin, and hence there can be no question that these varieties of disposition which have a more or less evident relation to the habits of life have been gradually induced and established in successive generations, and have become organic. That is to say, the tendencies to certain combinations of psychical changes have become organic. In the domesticated animals, parallel facts are familiar to all. Not only the forms and constitutions, but the habits of horses, oxen, sheep, pigs, and fowls, have become different from what they were in their wild state. In the various breeds of dogs, all of them according to the test of species derived from one stock, the varieties of mental character and faculty permanently established by mode of life, are numerous; and the several tendencies are spontaneously manifested. A young pointer will point at a covey the first time he in taken afield. A retriever brought up abroad, has been remarked to fulfil his duty without instruction. And in such cases the implication is that there is a bequeathed tendency for the psychical changes to take place in a special way. Even from the conduct of untamed creatures, we may gather some evidence having like implications. The birds of inhabited countries are far more difficult to approach than those of uninhabited ones. And the manifest inference is that continued experience of human enmity has produced an organic effect upon them—has modified their instincts—has modified the connections among their phychical states."

APPENDIX B.

* " The time was, so at least our grandmothers have told us, when our farmers' wives and daughters were models of healthy womanhood—fresh-cheeked, full-breasted, straight, lithe, active, and vigorous—worthy to be the wives and capable of becoming the mothers of strong, brave, large-hearted men. Such undoubtedly were the wives and mothers of Colonial and Revolutionary times, and such perhaps may be found now, but they are the exceptions to the prevailing pallor, debility and disease.

" The country girl is a favorite theme with the poet, and when she is what he generally paints her, she is more than worthy of his verse. What a picture of fresh and charming beauty does the mere mention of her name call up before the mind's eye! Those noble contours, that full and rounded bust, those sweet, frank, maidenly features; those deep, clear eyes, so full of sweet expression; those health-tinted cheeks, with their diffused and peachy bloom —all conspire to form a combination which no mortal man has either the power or the will to withstand. Such a being is a queen in her own right, and all men are her willing slaves. This is the ideal country girl—the country girl as

---

* " Hints towards Physical Perfection." By D. H. Jacques.

she ought to be and might be. Seek her among the corn fields and the orchards, and in the cottage homes which hide themselves among the apple trees! If you do not find her, you will find, in her place, the actual country girl of to-day, with perchance a crooked spine, a contracted chest, a diseased liver, and a dyspeptic stomach. Neuralgia, general debility, 'decline,' chlorosis, prolapsus uteri—the whole train of female diseases, in short, are now almost as common in the country as in the city. It is fashionable to be sentimentally pale ; to have 'delicate health ;' and alas ! to be consumptive and die young.

"How has the sound health and vital stamina of our grandmothers been lost ? The country air has not deteriorated ; pure water and sun light never fail, and have not lost their virtue ; the household duties of women are not more, but less severe ; wholesome food, or at least, the materials for making wholesome food are more abundant. Where, then, shall we look for the causes of the decay of health and beauty (for the latter goes with the former,) among the women of the country ?

"The foundations for it were perhaps laid in the very times of which our grandmothers boast, and in their own persons. They were full of vital stamina—vigorous and active ; but they had little or no assistance from servants or 'hired help' in their household labors—too severe even for them —which were scarcely remitted during gestation and lactation. The result, through the action of immutable laws, was deterioration to their offspring. Their daughters, less strong than themselves grew up to the same round of drudgery ; married in due time ; spent the months of maternal expectation in the kitchen, and in the performance of the rudest labors of the household ; and gave birth to their children (the expression is scarcely figurative) in the midst of their pots and kettles! A still further decadence was inevitable.

"Is it not strange that intelligent men—men, at least, who have long ago learned that dismissal from labor and extra care are required by their domestic animals during the period of gestation—remain still ignorant or careless of the fact that the same physiological laws apply still more imperatively, to the mothers of their children? Shame on the stupidity or brutality which fails to recognize and respect the sacred office of maternity, and to surround woman in the exercise of it, with the profoundest reverence and the most devoted and tender care."

"The woman about to become a mother," says Dr. Holmes, "or with her new-born infant upon her bosom, should be the object of trembling care and sympathy wherever she bears her tender burden or stretches her aching limbs. The very outcast in the streets has pity upon her sister in degradation when the seal of promised maternity is pressed upon her. The remorseless vengeance of the law brought down upon its victim by a machinery as sure as destiny, is arrested in its fall at a word which reveals her transient claim to mercy. The solemn prayer of the liturgy singles out her sorrows from the multiplied trials of life to plead for her in the hour of peril. God forbid that any member of the profession to which she trusts her life, doubly precious at that eventful period, should hazard it negligently, unadvisedly, or selfishly."

The preceeding eloquent passage was elicited on the occasion of demonstrating the eminently contagious nature of Puerperal Fever. "Well has Dr. Holmes said of those who, through a misunderstanding, or a misconception of the cause and character of this disease, have been the unintentional instruments of its spread and devastation :*—" No tongue can tell the heart-breaking calamity they have caused ; they have closed the eyes just opened upon a new world of love and happiness ; they have bowed the strength of manhood into the dust ; they have cast the helplessness of infancy into the stranger's arms, or bequeathed to it, with less cruelty, the death of its dying parent. There is no tone deep enough for regret, and no voice loud enough for warning."

The following extract from this author's 'Life of Goethe' corroborates his preceding views.

"Goethe's father was a cold, formal, stern, somewhat pedantic, but truth-loving, upright man. He hungered for knowledge, and although in general of a laconic turn, freely imparted all he learned. In his domestic circle his word was law. Not only imperious, but in some respects capricious, he was nevertheless greatly respected if little loved, by wife, children, and friends. He is characterized by Krause as 'a straight-forward Frankfort citizen,' whose habits were as measured as his gait. From him the poet inherited the well-built frame, the erect carriage, and the measured movement which in old age became stiffness, and was construed into diplomacy or haughtiness ; from him also came that orderliness and stoicism which have so much distressed those who cannot characterize genius otherwise than as vagabond in its habits, the lust for knowledge, the delight in communicating it, the almost pedantic attention to details which are noticeable in the poet, are all traceable in the father.

"The mother was more like what we conceive as the pro

---

* Journal of National Medicine. Edited by C. H. Cleveland, M D., of Cincinnati.

per parent for a poet. She is one of the pleasantest figures in German literature, and one standing out with greater vividness than almost any other. Her simple, hearty, joyous, and affectionate nature, endeared her to all. She was the delight of children, the favorite of poets and princes. To the last retaining her enthusiasm and simplicity, mingled with great shrewdness and knowledge of character, *Frau Aga*, as they christened her, was at once grave and hearty, dignified and simple. She had read most of the best German and Italian authors, had picked up considerable desultory information, and had that 'mother wit' which so often seems to render culture superfluous in women, their rapid intuitions anticipating the tardy conclusions of experience— a characteristic also of the poetic mind. Her letters are full of spirit; not always strictly grammatical, not irreproachable in orthography, but vigorous with vivacity. After a lengthened interview with her, an enthusiastic traveler says, 'Now do I understand how Goethe has become the man he is!' Wieland, Merck, Burger, Madame de Stael, Karl August, and other great people, sought her acquaintance. The Duchess Amelia corresponded with her as with an intimate friend; a letter from her was a small jubilee at the Weimar Court. She was married at seventeen to a man she did not love, and was only eighteen when the poet was born. This, instead of making her prematurely old, seems to have perpetuated her girlhood. 'I and my Wolfgang,' she said, 'have always held fast to each other, because we are both young together.' To him she transmitted her love of story-telling, her animal spirits, her love of every thing that bore the stamp of distinctive individuality, and her love of seeing happy faces around her. 'Order and quiet,' she says in one of her charming letters to Freiherr von Stein, 'are my principal characteristics. Hence I dispatch at once whatever I have to do, the most disagreeable always first, and I gulp down the devil without looking at him. When all has returned to its proper state then I defy any one to surpass me in good humor.' Her heartiness and tolerance are the causes, she thinks, why every one likes her. I am fond of people, and *that* every one feels directly—young and old. I pass without pretension through the world, and that gratifies men. I never *bemoralize* any one—*always seek out the good that is in them*—and leave all that is bad to Him who made mankind, and knows how to round off the angles. In this way I make myself happy and comfortable.' Who does not recognise the son in those accents? The kindliest of men inherited his loving, happy nature from the heartiest of women.'

APPENDIX C.

"In the growth of civilization," says H. W. Beecher, "women have steadily risen, and have enlarged their sphere and multiplied their functions. May we not reasonably expect that hereafter the same development will proceed? Are there not for woman, as for man, new applications of power, new spheres of influence? Or is man the true fruit of the human race, and woman only a blossom, good to give him a start, then to perish, and let him swell to full proportion?

"Consider the lesson of history. How much has woman advanced in variety of functions and in versatility of powers! She was once an article of merchandise, and is still, among savages. She was secluded, and not accounted an equal member, even among her own family. Her name in many nations has been a synonym for all that is weak, vain and contemptible. She has been, in some periods of the world, denied the rights of social life; and, by arguments just such as are now employed to bar her further usefulness, it has been declared that she ought not to be educated, that her province was subordinate, and her duty the service of the coarser man. The educated woman of our days would have been the wonder of early civilizations. She has attained and holds without remark a degree of liberty and various efficiency which would have violated the customs and shocked the prejudices of olden days. At each change, at every upward step, have stood these pleaders, whose undegenerate posterity are yet in the same manner reasoning, affirming that already she was in her right place, and should stay where Providence placed her. For the men who reason with faces prone to the earth think always that the state to which the world has grown to this day is all that God meant it should ever grow. Men of great conceit have ever thought that Time was ripe in them. At length woman dawned into literature, and changed the spirit of letters. When she became a reader man no longer wrote as if for men. She enforced purity and higher decorum. When woman came as a reader and a writer, then again men, saw that guiding star which led them where the young child of Christian purity lay. For, after all, it is the pen that is the tongue of the world, and a woman's hand is becoming more influential than the orator's mouth.

"Woman has also advanced to a higher sphere as a teacher, and all are beginning to feel, although it does not appear what she is to do, that a new life is opened to her. Thus, step by step, against prejudices and arguments of her unfitness, against rude pushes downwards, and much advice as to her proper duties, (which in the main have been the drudgeries that men disliked,) woman has advanced to a wider plane, to higher duties, to a liberty of following freely her own natural gifts, and to the reluctant recognition of her right to do whatever she could do well!

"Nor have the prophecies that, like bats, flitted about her, been fulfilled. In the augmentation of her liberty an the enlargement of her sphere she has forsaken no duty of home, and lost no grace of tenderness and love. She has become a better mother, wife, daughter, sister, friend, by just that enlargement which it was predicted, would unsex her. Experience has shown that as women are made to be worth more to society at large, and in public interests, they are worth more at home, and are capable of building *it* better, and administering its duties and affections more skilfully and refinedly. Woman is not best in the family in communities where she is the most secluded. She is richest in all household excellencies in those societies where she has liberty of widest activity and motives to the exercise of her tatents upon the largest scale. That vulgar maxim, worn smooth in fools' mouths, that a woman ought to stay at home and take care of her husband's clothes and her children's food, is a switch cut from the great tree of Arrogance under which despotic men have always sat, and from which the strong have always cut their bludgeons and cudgels wherewith to strike down or chastise the weak. A woman is better fitted for home who is also fit for something else. It is largeness, it is generous culture, it is power made skilful by exercise, that make both men and women rich in domestic life. Whatever makes her a better thinker, a larger-minded actor, a deeper thoughted observer, a more potent writer or teacher, makes her by just so much a better wife and mother. No one is a better friend for being ignorant. No one is a more tender companion for being weak and helpless, Our homes demand great hearts and strong hands; but these need the culture of open air and the free heavens. They are not of the hot-bed or the conservatory."

"Right position of women in a state," says Emerson, " is another index of civilization. Poverty and industry with a healthy mind read very easily the laws of humanity, and love them : place the sexes in right relations of mutual respect, and a severe morality gives that essential charm to woman which educates all that is delicate, poetic and self-sacrificing, breeds courtesy and learning, conversation and wit, in her rough mate ; so that I have thought it a sufficient definition of civilization to say, it is the influence of good women."

"Hitherto," says Theodore Parker, " with woman circumstances have hindered the development of intellectual power in all its forms. She has not knowledge or practical skill to equal the power of man. But circumstances have favored the development of pure and lofty emotions in advance of man. She has moral feeling, affectional feeling, religious feeling, far in advance of man ; her moral, affectional, and religious intuitions are deeper and more trustworthy than his. Here she is eminent, as he is in knowledge, in ideas, in administrative skill.

"I think man will always lead in affairs of intellect, of reason, imagination, understanding — he has the bigger brain ; but that woman will always lead in affairs of emotion —moral, affectional, religious—she has the better heart, the truer intuition of the right, the lovely, the holy. The literature of women in this country is juster, more philanthropic, more religious than that of men. Do you not hear the cry which in New England a woman is raising in the world's ears against the foul wrong which America is working in the world ? Do you not hear the echo of that woman's voice come over the Atlantic, returned from European shores in many a tongue—French, German, Italian, Swedish, Danish, Russian, Dutch ? How a woman touches the world's heart, because she speaks justice, piety and love. . . . . Man's moral action at least is only a sort of general human providence, aiming at the welfare of a part, and satisfied with achieving the 'greatest good of the greatest number.' Woman's moral action is more like a human providence, acting without general rules, but caring for each particular case. We need both of these, the general and the special, to make a total providence."

APPENDIX D.

The following summary of woman's influence in improving modern literature, and refining society, is from the pen of one of the most profound thinkers and ripest of scholars of the age,—it reflects credit on both head and heart.*

"Full justice has never been done to the influence of woman on literature and society. Neither the classic nor the feudal age had anything deserving to be called society. What we call by that name was born in modern times, and owes its existence to woman. Society, the natural out-growth of the New Testament, without which Christianity was only a dogma, a hermit, or a monster,—was never born till woman was allowed her true place, and man learned that really under Christ, there was neither male nor female,—society, the only field where the sexes have ever met on terms of equality—the arena where character is formed and studied—the crucible of ideas—the cradle and the realm of public opinion—the spur and crown of ambition—the world's university—the tribunal which unmasks pretension and stamps real merit—at once a school and a theatre—which gives government leave to be, and outruns the formal church in guiding the moral sense of the age,—who shall fitly tell us

---
* Wendell Philips.

the power of this marvelous agent over the civil and religious world? What else can so rightfully claim the first place among the controlling elements of the last two centuries? Yet this is the throne of woman; the throne which, like a first conqueror, she founded and then filled. * * * "The wealth of a nation's literature comes mostly from many rills that pour tribute into the central sea. Each one sees the great objects of human thought from a different stand-point, as colored by class, position, mood, sex, relation, history and hope. When *sensation* passes into *thought* and *images* become *impressions* they put on the hue of the blood that gives them life; and thus each thinker is in fact, a fresh Adam, with a new creation spread out before him. Hitherto the man, father, son, hero, tyrant, cold, intellectual, defiant, scrutinizing, has reflected for us the images of the universe. Now the mother, wife, impulse, affection, instinct, love of right, impatience of compromise, taste, duty that not only will not heed but does not see consequences,—these look at God's world for us. I dare to say, that from this single cause, modern literature is richer than the ancient in original ideas; richer and growing more so every day, because woman is the audience writers address; and woman is herself a writer, revealing her own impressions and soul. * * * In just so far as woman is eternally different from man, in just that degree will thought refracted through her nature, come flashing forth in a thousand new colors. As well plant yourself in a desert, under the changeless gray and blue, and assert that you have seen all the wonders of God's pencil, as maintain that a male literature, Latin, Greek, or Asiatic, can be anything but a half part, one sided, poor and awry. As well develope only muscle, shutting out sunshine and color, and starving flesh from your angular limbs, and then advise men to scorn Titian's flesh and the Apollo, since you have exhausted manly beauty,—as well think to stir all the depths of music with only half the chords. The diapason of human thought was never struck, till Christian culture summoned woman into the republic of letters; and nature as well as experience tells us, 'what God hath joined, let no man put asunder.' Whether you take modern novels, filling so large a space in our modern literature,—the child of society, and breathing only in its atmosphere,—or history in its grandest reach, or the profoundest research of philosophical or social thought, it would be easy to point out the marked influence of the presence or the memory of woman in making our writers differ from all who preceded them. * * * Four hundred years ago, with only here and there an exception, no woman touched a pen. To-day we are rid of one half of this absurd injustice. Woman is part of the great social organization; she thinks, she writes, she reads, she is a part of the motive force of the century. And, mark me! the literature of four centuries ago, when woman was not a reader, is gross, obscene, below the level of decent recognition; men must expurgate in order to print it. Woman has become a reader, and literature springs to a higher level. It must always be so, in all cases, where the two sexes harmoniously take part. . . . It is no longer a question whether she shall shape the policy of the age; she shares now the throne in that veiled, but omnipotent realm, where the moral sense and public opinion are formed. She has the pen in her right hand, and these material bodies of ours, though you count them by millions, are the servants of one soul, upon whose brow God puts the invisible circlet of mental sovereignty. * * * If we have the Somervilles, and Nightingales, Edgworths, and Charlotte Brontes, and George Sands, and the other great women mentioned in the literature of this century, it is in vain to say, that we men must not bend to genius, when God touches its lips!"

APPENDIX E.

"From the fact that the human race is in a state of transition, we may suspect that the existing ratio between its ability to multiply and its ability to maintain life, is not a constant ratio. From the fact that its fertility is at present in excess of what is needed, we may infer that any change in the ratio will probably be toward a diminution of fertility. And from the fact that on the whole civilization increases the ability to maintain life, we may perceive that there is at work some influence by which such diminution is necessitated. Before inquiring for this influence, let us consider in what directions an increase of ability to maintain life may take—what scope there is for an increase. In some further development of the co-ordinating system, that is in some greater co-ordination of actions, the increase must of course consist. But there are several kinds of co-ordination ; and it would be well to ask of what kind or kinds increase is most requisite, and therefore most likely. For doubtless in conformity with the general law of adaptation, increase will take place only where it is demanded.

"Will it be in strength? Probably not. Though from prehistoric remains, we may gather that the race has become more bulky, yet the cause of this change seems now diminishing. Mechanical appliances are fast supplanting muscular force, and will most likely continue to do so until they leave to be done by manual labor only as much as is needful for the healthy maintenance of the body at its then attained size.

Will it be in swiftness or agility? Probably not. In the savage these form important elements of the ability to maintain life; but in the civilized man they subserve that end in quite a minor degree, and there seems no circumstance likely to necessitate an increase of them.

"Will it be in mechanical skill, that is, in the co-ordination of complex movements? Most likely in some degree. Awkwardness is continually entailing injuries and loss of life. Moreover, the complicated tools developed by civilization are constantly requiring greater delicacy of manipulation. Already the cerebellum, which is the nervous centre directing compound motions, is larger in man than in any other creature except the elephant; and the daily-increasing variety and complexity of the processes he has to perform, and the appliances he has to use, may be expected to cause a further growth of it.

"Will it be in intelligence? Largely, no doubt. There is ample room for progress in this direction, and ample demand for it. Our lives are universally shortened by our ignorance. In attaining complete knowledge of our own nature, and the nature of surrounding things—in ascertaining the conditions of existence to which we must conform, and in discovering means of conforming to them under all variations of seasons and circumstances—we have abundant scope for intellectual culture, and urgent need for intellectual development.

"Will it be in morality, that is, in greater power of self-regulation? Largely, also; perhaps most largely. Normal conduct, or in other words, conduct conducive to the maintenance of perfect and long-continued life, is usually come short of more from defect of will than from knowledge. To the due co-ordination of those complex actions which constitute human life in its civilized form, there goes not only the pre-requisite—recognition of the proper course, but the further pre-requisite—a due impulse to pursue that course. And on calling to mind our daily failure to fulfil often-repeated resolutions, we shall perceive that lack of the needful desire rather than lack of insight, is the chief cause of faulty action. A further endowment of those feelings which civilization is developing in us—sentiments responding to the requirements of the social state—emotive faculties that find their gratifications in the duties devolving on us—must be acquired before the crimes, excesses, diseases, improvidences, dishonesties and cruelties that now so greatly diminish the duration of life, can cease.

" But whether co-ordination of actions take place in any or in all of these directions, and in whatever degree or proportions, it is clear that if it take place at all, it must be at the expense of fertility. Regarded from the abstract point of view, increased ability to maintain life in this case, as in all others, necessarily involves decreased ability to multiply. Or, regarded in the concrete, that further development in the co-ordinating system any advance presupposes, implies further decrease in the production of co-ordinating cells.

" That an enlargement of the nervous centers is going on in mankind, is an ascertained fact. Not alone from a general survey of human progress—not alone from the greater power of self-preservation shown by civilized races, are we left to infer such enlargement; it is proved by actual measurement. The mean capacities of the crania in the leading divisions of the species have been found to be—

" In the Australian, 75 cubic inches,
 " African, 82 "
 " Malayan, 86 "
 " Englishman, 96* "

* Lecture by Prof. Owen before Zoological Society, Nov. 11, 1851,

showing an increase in the course of the advance from the savage state to our present phase of civilization, amounting to nearly thirty per cent. on the original size. That this increase will be continuous might be reasonably assumed, and to infer a future decrease of fertility would be tolerably safe were no further evidence forthcoming. But it may be shown why a greater development of the nervous system must take place, and why, consequently, there must be a diminution of the present excess of fertility, and further, it may be shown that the sole agency needed to work out this change is—*the excess of fertility itself.*

"For as we all know, this excess of fertility entails a pressure of population upon the means of subsistence; and, as long as it exists, must continue to do this. Looking only at the present and the immediate future, it is unquestionably true that if unchecked, the rate of increase of people would exceed the rate of increase of food. It is clear the wants of their redundant numbers constitute the only stimulus mankind have to a greater production of the necessaries of life, for, were not the demand beyond the supply, there would be no motive to increase the supply. Moreover, this excess of demand over supply, and this pressure of population, of which it is the index, cannot be eluded. Though by the emigration that takes place when the pressure arrives at a certain intensity, a partial and temporary relief may be obtained, yet, as by this process all the habitable countries must gradually become peopled, it follows, that in the end the pressure, whatever it may then be, must be borne in full.

" But this redundancy of numbers—this constant increase of people beyond the means of subsistence—involving as it does an increasing stimulus to better the modes of producing food and other necessaries—involves also an increasing demand for skill, intelligence, and self-control—involves, therefore, a constant exercise of these, that is, involves a gradual growth of them. Every improvement is at once the product of a higher form of humanity, and demands that higher form of humanity to carry it into practice. The application of science to the arts is simply the bringing to bear greater intelligence for satisfying our wants, and implies continued increase of that intelligence. To get more product from the acre, the farmer must study chemistry—must adopt new mechanical appliances—and must, by the application of tools and processes, cultivate both his own powers and the powers of his laborers. To meet the requirements of the market, the manufacturer is perpetually improving his old machines, and inventing new ones; and by the premium of high wages incites artisans to acquire greater skill. The daily widening ramifications of commerce entail upon the merchant a need for more knowledge and more complex calculations; while the lessening profits of the ship owner force him to employ greater science in building, to get captains of higher intelligence, and better crews. In all cases increase of numbers is the efficient cause. Were it not for the competition this entails, more thought would not daily be brought to bear upon the business of life; greater activity of mind would not be called for; and development of mental power would not take place. Difficulty in getting a living is alike the incentive to a higher educacation of children, and to a more intense and long-continued application in adults. In the mother it induces foresight, economy, and skillful housekeeping; in the father, laborious days and constant self-denial. Nothing but necessity could make men submit to this discipline and nothing but this discipline could produce a continued progression. The contrast between a Pacific Islander, all whose wants are supplied by nature, and an Englishman, who, generation after generation, has had to bring to the satisfaction of his wants ever increasing knowledge and skill, illustrates at once the need for, and the effects of such discipline. And this being admitted, it cannot be denied that a further continuance of such discipline, possibly under a yet more intense form, must produce a further progress in the same direction—a further enlargement of the nervous centers, and a further decline of fertility.

" And here it must be remarked, that the effect of pressure of population, in increasing the ability to maintain life, and decreasing the ability to multiply, is not a uniform effect, but an average one. In this case as in many others, nature secures each step in advance by a succession of trials; which are perpetually repeated, and cannot fail to be repeated, until success is achieved. All mankind in turn, subject themselves more or less to the discipline described; they either may or may not advance under it; but in the nature of things, only those who *do* advance under it eventually survive. For, necessarily, families and races whom this increasing difficulty of getting a living which excess of fertility entails, does not stimulate to improvements in production—that is, to greater mental activity—are on the high road to extinction; and must ultimately be supplanted by those whom the pressure does so stimulate. This truth we have recently seen exemplified in Ireland. And here, indeed, without further illustration, it will be seen that premature death, under all its forms, and from all its causes, cannot fail to work in the same direction. For as those prematurely carried off must, in the average of cases, be those in whom the power of self-preservation is the least, it unavoidably follows, that those left behind to continue the race are those in whom the power of self-preservation is the greatest—are the select of their generation. So that whether the damages to existence be of the kind produced by excess of fertility, or of any other kind, it is clear that by the ceaseless exercise of the faculties needed to contend with them, and by the death of all men who fail to contend with them successfully, there is insured a constant progress toward a higher degree of skill, intelligence, and self-regulation—a better co-ordination of actions—a more complete life.

"There now remains but to inquire toward what limit this progress tends. Evidently, so long as the fertility of the race is more than sufficient to balance the diminution by deaths, population continues to increase; so long as population continues to increase, there must be pressure on the means of subsistence; and so long as there is pressure on the means of subsistence, further mental development must go on, and further diminution of fertility must result. Hence the change can never cease until the rate of multiplication is just equal to the rate of mortality; that is, can never cease until, on the average, each pair brings to maturity but two children. Probably this involves that each pair will rarely produce more than two offspring; seeing that with the greatly increased ability to preserve life, which the hypothesis presupposes, the amount of infant and juvenile mortality must become small. Be this as it may, however, it is manifest that, in the end, pressure of population and its accompanying evils will entirely disappear; and will leave a state of things which will require from each individual no more than a normal and pleasurable activity. That this inference is a legitimate corollary will become obvious on a little consideration. For, a cessation in the decrease of fertility implies a cessation in the development of the nervous system; and this implies that the nervous system has become fully equal to all that is demanded of it—has not to do more than is natural to it. But that exercise of faculties which does not exceed what is natural constitutes gratification. Consequently in the end, the obtainment of subsistence will require just that kind and that amount of action needful to perfect health and happiness.

"Thus do we see how simple are the means by which the greatest and most complex results are worked out. From the point of view now reached, it becomes plain that the necessary antagonism of individuation and reproduction not only fulfills with precision the *à priori* law of maintenance of race, from the monad up to man, but insures the final attainment of the highest form of this maintenance—a form in which the amount of life shall be the greatest possible, and the births and deaths the fewest possible. In the nature of things the antagonism could not fail to work out the results we see it working out. The gradual diminution and ultimate disappearance of the original excess of fertility could take place only through the process of civilization; and at the same time, the excess of fertility has itself rendered the process of civilization inevitable. From the begining pressure of population has been the proximate cause of progress. It produced the original diffusion of the race. It compelled men to abandon predatory habits and take to agriculture. It led to clearing the earth's surface. It forced men into the social state; made social organization inevitable; and has developed the social sentiments. It has stimulated to progressive improvements in production, and to increased skill and intelligence. It is daily pressing us into closer contact and more mutually dependent relationships. And after having caused, as it ultimately must, the due peopling of the globe, and the bringing of all its habitable parts into the highest state of culture—after having brought all processes for the satisfaction of human wants to the greatest perfection—after having at the same time, developed the intellect into competency for its work, and the feelings into complete fitness for social life—after having done all this, we see that the pressure of population, as it gradually finishes its work, must gradually bring itself to an end."

APPENDIX F.

"THE great embarrassment to social progress, the one obstacle to a more equitable distribution of wealth, is the general neglect of any prudential restraint upon population. Those who exclaim against this doctrine are either the ornamental class who deliberately desire the mass of the population should remain in poverty that they themselves may live in splendor and idleness, or weak-headed sentimentalists with whom feeling—and that not very refined—takes the place of reason. To the former we say nothing. They at least know what they are about. To the latter we recommend a calm perusal of Mr. Mill's admirable examinination of 'Low Wages and their Remedies.' If they remain unconvinced by his demonstrations, they are not fit to be argued with."—North British Review.

"To the unionist the population question is all-important. At present he must not expect any concession from the employer which he is not in a position to enforce. A moral change we are told may take place in the capitalist. Granted; but his heart will melt much more rapidly when he has been chastened, to borrow the language of the pulpit, in the furnace of affliction. He will begin to doubt the morality of his position, when its policy has become an open question. * * * Remove from him the temptation which the weakness and isolation of the laborer offers, and his notions of right and wrong will be wonderfully altered. But the laboring class as a whole will never be able to treat with the capitalist class on equal terms, as long as it continues to populate without regard to the state of the labor market. Here and there a body of men by rigid combinations—by disentangling themselves as it were from the struggling and sinking mass, might manage to maintain their position; but the general tendency would be inevitably downwards.

"There is no shirking this difficulty. The fate of the working-classes is in their own hands. So simple is the proof, that had they but one mind to be persuaded, one will to be influenced, the victory were already won. The inference is obvious. Combination is not unity, but it is something like it. As long as a man knows that all self-denial on his part will be neutralized by some one less public-spirited than himself, he will not forego what he regards as, after all, a legitimate satisfaction. Whether the object be to obtain a concession from an employer or to check population, the one necessity for working men is to know whether they can depend upon one another.

"We do not despair. Although plenty of men are to be found in every rank of life who recklessly produce families which they have no means of supporting, there are only two classes of whom it can be said, that such shameless selfishness is the rule rather than the exception—the agricultural paupers and the clergy of the Established Church. Both these classes abdicate all responsibility, and are content to leave the prospects of their offspring to chance or charity. Among the skilled mechanics earning comfortable wages, there is, we believe, something more of prudence and self-respect; but it is hardly to be expected that improvement in this respect will become general, so long as public opinion looks leniently upon conduct as degrading as it is anti-social. At present if an artisan limits his family within reasonable bounds it is for reasons that concern only himself, and those dependent on him. He objects to diminish his comforts; he thinks it his duty to give his children a fair start in life, he desires to exempt his wife from the miserable drudgery which a large and constantly increasing family entails. All these motives deserve the highest respect; but regard for the interests of his class would be a still nobler principle of action. Everything leads him to view his class as a whole, possessing common objects and common interests,—everything which accustoms him to sacrifice his individual tastes and inclinations, when they conflict with the well-being of the whole body, must tend to force this momentous question on his attention. It is combination alone which will bring him face to face with the great difficulty of the social problem. When once he feels that to be the parent of an immoderately large family is, in the eyes of his fellows, a selfish and unjustifiable draught on the common fund, he will shrink from incurring their well-merited censure. It is not too much, therefore, to expect that trades' unions will eventually prove a check on the increase of population, and so confer an important benefit on society at large."—Stuart Mill's Political Economy.

APPENDIX G.

Among the varied aspects which the question of a prudential check on population assumes, one is to be found in the following extract from a recent work of Dr. Hall on "Sleep." The book contains many valuable suggestions on this, and kindred subjects.

"The plan of this book is to show the destructive influence on health and life which bad air exercises; to state a variety of causes of deterioration, among which the most rapid in their effects are emanations from the human body, and the expirations from the lungs; and therefore, as we spend a third of our existence in sleep, during which, in consequence of its passive condition, the corporeal system is greatly more liable to the influence of the causes of disease, it is of the utmost consequence that every practical and rational means for securing a pure air for the chamber should be employed, the most important of these being large rooms and single beds.

"It is not only unwise, it is unnatural and degenerative, for one person to pass the night habitually in the same bed or room with another, whatever may be the age, sex, or relationship of the parties. Unwise, because it impairs the general health and undermines the constitution, by reason of the fact, that the atmosphere of any ordinary chamber occupied by more than one sleeper, is speedily vitiated, and that in this vitiated condition, it is breathed over and over again for the space of the eight hours usually passed in sleep, amounting in the aggregate, to one-third of a man's entire existence. Unnatural, because it is contrary to our instincts; and it is lowering, because it dimishes that mutual consideration and respect which ought to prevail in social life. A person feels elevated in proportion to the deference received from another, and there springs up a self-restraint, a consciousness of personal dignity, which has an exalting effect on the whole physical, moral, and social nature of man; but the habitual occupation of the same chamber must largely detract from these in a variety of ways.

"A conjectural reason forms another argument against two persons sleeping near each other. Each individual has an amount of electrical influence, which in its normal proportion, is health to him. Electricity, like air and water, tends constantly to an equilibrium, and when two bodies come near each other, having different quantities, that which has the greatest imparts to that which has the least, until both are equal. The lightning and the thunder are caused by this exchange between a cloud which has plus, and another has its share, minus. Wind is the passing of air from a section which has more to another which has less. But if a human body with its healthful share of electricity or other influence, gives part of it to another which has less, it gives away just that much of its life. and must die, unless it is recovered in some way; hence the frequent fact, which it needs no authority to substantiate, that a healthy young infant, who sleeps with an old person, will wither and wilt and wane and die. Thus also, the healthy have been observed to grow diseased themselves, by sleeping with sickly persons.

"In the author's experience, of some twenty years, in the special study and treatment of common consumption of the lungs, the fact has stood out with constant confirmation, that of the widows and widowers applying for relief, quite a large proportion had lost their companions by consumption.

"On the other hand no fact has come to light as yet, which proves that the more weak or sickly person is at all benefited by what injures the healthier party.

"If, then, two clouds of different electrical states cannot approach each other without a mutual change of conditions, and if man, who has an electrical state natural and healthful to him, comes near another in an unhealthful state, it would seem demonstrative that harm, by an unchangeable physical law, must fall to the healthier without benefiting the other; and that sleeping together in the same bed is a certain injury, and ought to be avoided as a habit by every reflecting person who is so fortunate as to have the means of having a room and a bed to himself. It certainly is undeniable, that influences are exchanged, call them what we may, which waste away the life of the child, and make it wither and wilt and die, like a flower without water. The same is true of the robust sleeping with the weakly, and the feeble sleeping with the strong. This interchange of influence from close association is such, that in the course of years the man and wife have been taken for brother and sister. But it is a law of nature enforced by authority, human and divine, that blood-relations shall not intermarry; observation shows that it deteriorates the race morally, mentally, and physically This may point to the fact that human health, that is, the perfection of our physical nature, at least its preservation, is dependent to a great extent on intermarriages between persons who are as great a remove as possible from one another, and we may say, of electrical states as different as possible. It must be confessed that this is conjecture as to the system—but the one fact is clear, that sleeping together in the same bed is destructive to health as between the old and the young, as between the well and the sick, and we may infer as between persons of different constitutions, as in the case of man and wife. Divinity has wisely ordered that the preservation and perpetuation of the race should depend on the gratification of certain appetites and propensities, and that such gratifications should be pleasurable. But a high wisdom dictates that these should not be blunted by immoderate indulgence, nor marred by too frequent repetition; and it should be remembered that they are all under the same general laws, for infinite wisdom avoids unnecessary complications and diversities. 'Few and simple,' may be considered the description of all the regulations necessary for the preservation of corporeal man. 'Regularity and moderation,' is written on all that gives us pleasure, with a wise view that it should wear out only with life, and that at a good old age. The regulations connected with eating, drinking, sleeping, etc. are so much alike, the temptation to over-indulge so constant, the necessity of restraint so apparent, and the evils of excess as to times and amounts so much to be dreaded, that a volume might be filled in illustrating each. It may, however, suffice to treat only of one or two, leaving it to the intelligence and aptness of the reader to make a general application, and thus much time and space will be saved, while the practical lessons will be equally valuable.

"Instinct is given to the brute, but diviner reason to man; the great aim and end of both being the preservation and perpetuation of the species of each. This instinct and reason were implanted for the purpose of regulating the enjoyment of those pleasures which are wisely and benevolently made a happiness and a necessity. Instinct leads the brute to the indulgence of the appetites, and how often and how much it shall eat and drink, and sleep is apportioned in a manner which makes excess impracticable; hence there is a happy exemption from the million forms of disease and pain and suffering belonging to the lot of man. He was made of a nobler nature, and treated as a nobleman, in that he was not bound down by rules and regulations as inflexible as fetters of brass, but was left to govern himself, to choose for himself, to act for himself, with the reward of elevation here and happiness hereafter, if he deport himself well; but with the penalty of suffering and death, physical and moral, if he failed to practice a high and a wise and a dignified self-restraint, the first element of which, as to eating, drinking and sleeping, is uniformity. A certain amount of sleep rests, renews and strengthens the whole man, but to accomplish such a result, sleep must be regular. As to what constitutes regularity, it is only necessary to remark, that the general habit should be to retire at the same hour in the early evening of every day. In a short time the result will be an ability to go to sleep within a few moments after retiring, and to sleep continually until morning, provided the sleeper leaves his bed the moment he first wakes up, and does not sleep during the day. In this way sleep will be refreshing, will be delicious, and to the busy worker of the brain or the body, will be worth more than silver or gold, and this priceless habit of sleeping soundly will be continued to a good old age.

"It is in one sense a daily miracle that a man wakes up out of sleep; the more it is considered the more wonderful will it appear. With a regularity of retirement, and arranging to guard against interruptions, nature wakes us up the very moment the system has had enough repose—the propensity will come on within a few minutes of the regular time, will grow stronger until it is yielded to, and eventually will become in a measure irresistible, or its resistance will be attended with great discomfort. Another result will be, that the body will wake up from sleep within a few minutes of the same point of time, from one month's end to another, being a little sooner or later, making variations according to the temperature of the weather, the condition of the atmosphere, and the amount of the exercise of the preceding day. Thus it is with other desires of the animal nature. Let there be an appointed time, not to be changed for any common reason; the feelings will come at that appointed time, and when satisfied, nature calls for no more until the appointed time comes round again.

"But suppose enough sleep is not given. Suppose we make an effort to rob nature of her due allowance, madness, unending and hopeless is the result; if the curtailment is not great, various degrees of debility and wasting and decline come on apace.

"Suppose, on the other hand, it is attempted to force more sleep on nature than she requires, it is an unnatural sleep, it does not rest and refresh and invigorate; and instead of having more good sleep, the whole of it is restless and disturbed, and we lose the lusciousness of it all.

"As to eating there is a remarkable parallel If a man eats when he is decidedly hungry, and at regular hours of the day, not stimulating or teasing or tempting the appetite by a great variety of food or otherwise, he will be regularly hungry under ordinary circumstances, will digest his food well, and will not desire it especially, except at the stated times.

"If, on the other hand, the appetite is stimulated, if it is tempted, or if a person places himself in a situation where food can be had for the turning around, or for the stretching out of the hand, and it is taken when there is no special desire for it, and when the person would just as soon let it alone as to take it, under these circumstances a fictitious appetite will be created, the digestion will be deranged, a depraved craving for food will be set up, but no sooner will it be swallowed, than some troublesome feeling will arise, only to be arrested by another gratification; and thus the whole life is a craving, an unsatisfied desire, and so much of a burden that the predominating wish is to die.

"In this same manner have multitudes fallen from high positions into degrading habits of beastly intoxication, by allowing themselves to have convenient drinks at hand, and at first to taste them, not for any particular relish, but just to be doing something; and having no regular hours for drink, and no regular quantity, an unnatural desire springs up, a steady craving is generated, increasing in its remorselessness day by day, until there is no happiness but in constant indulgence, when even that ceases to satisfy, and life is a torture.

"The appetites, then, are to be gratified at stated times, and at none other. They are not to be teased or tempted or stimulated by always having at hand the facilities for gratification but kept in abeyance for fixed occasions; those occasions being determined at first by the decided calls of nature, which will then be made regularly, moderately, and continuously, to the end of life.

"But if the means of gratification are kept at hand, if the mind is permitted to rest on them and cherish them, to look forward to them, to tempt, to tease, to worry, the inevitable result will be a morbid appetite, a voracious craving never to be satisfied, energies wasted, powers prostrated, and an early and irretrievable decay, inducing, in a greater multitude of cases than one would imagine, a depressed and soured life and a miserable suicide's grave. If the victim survives incessant tortures, life is a drawn out agony. Inordinate indulgence wastes away the physical constitution, the influence of which is perpetuated to all that is born of it; throwing around the hapless victim the coils of a boa-constrictor, which are tightened pitilessly every day, until health, and hope, and life itself, mortal and immortal, are crushed out helplessly and forever.

"What is said of real but unlawful indulgences, is true of all forms of the artificial; and excesses in the lawful are not the less pernicious, are not the less destructive to body and health, to heart and soul, than are excesses in the unnatural and the unlawful; and in this statement there is a lesson of the very highest practical importance to every reader; hence the pains taken in these pages to convince the understanding, that as to the appetites of our nature, barriers should be opposed to the too inordinate and too facile opportunities of gratification; and that as to them all, there should be such metes and bounds as the nobler reason may indicate, and as observation and experience may show are proper, healthful and safe. Without wise restraints, as experienced physicians well know, effects unsuspected by the sufferers themselves, or by their friends, are sometimes induced, which have a deplorable influence on mind and body; as to the latter wearing it away into hopeless emaciation and decline; and as to the mind, inducing an exaggeration of many of the most undesirable charateristics of our nature; it becomes unsteady, vacillating, fretful, morose and suspicious; self-respect and self-esteem are lost; an intolerable depression weighs down the whole man; hope, desire and ambition fail, and relief is mostly sought in suicide, the sorrowful verdict being, 'died by his own hand;' a verdict rendered oftener than many think for, over the doubly dishonored body; dishonored in the manner of the death, and more deeply still by the degrading causes of it.

"Such being some of the results of over-indulgences, thoughtful persons naturally seek for some rule of guidance, and we are not left without an index, without some friendly line of right and safety. Revelation seems to mark out that line, interposes a mete and bound, decides the measure of our gratifications in the comprehensive expressions· 'Be ye temperate in all things.' 'Let your moderation be known to all.' If this temperance is not observed, if this moderation is not practiced habitually, persistently, and with a wise noble heroic self-denial, the penalty will not fail to be inflicted, pleasure will first lose its keenness, next it will pall upon the senses, and ultimately fail. In one direction sleep has been lost; in another the appetite for food has been lost; and the person becomes the victim of ills, physical, mental and moral, which makes of life a crushing burden, a miserable failure, a continued curse.

"It is to the excessive indulgence of the appetite which leisure and easy opportunity affords in large cities, that family names die out so soon. It is rare in Paris, that the grandchild reaches manhood in vigorous health, if at all, whose parents and grandparents were born and lived and died in that voluptuous capital. The rapid disappearance of family names which were prominent and numerous in New York in the begining of the present century, shows that the greatest city in the New World is not behind the greatest of the Old, in the respect named; not owing wholly, it is true, to extravagant indulgences, but largely owing to that, beyond contradiction.

"In every direction, idleness and opportunity have led multitudes everywhere, in the city and in the country to brutalize themselves. For example, one very common cause of some of the worst forms of dyspeptic disease is, the not being particularly engaged, while at the same time, some inviting article of food is at hand in the same room. This has been already referred to; it is the same in relation to drink, and every other form of indulgence, and there is no safety against any of them, but in the interposition of efficient barriers to too facile gratifications, and the more of these a man can erect, the safer will he be, and they are wise, who use all means for the purpose which can even slightly aid in accomplishing the result.

"The reflecting reader can here form the requisite rules of action ; the first great laws being regularity and temperance ; the latter being promoted by not having at hand the easy opportunity of indulgence ; by putting temptation out of the way; by cultivating an active and fully occupied life, and by not making it his chief aim and end, to eat and drink and enjoy the pleasures which perish in the moment of their using, but to live for the high and absorbing purpose of human elevation and of achieving an immortal existence beyond the present scenes. Sight and propinquity, and touch bring wants which otherwise would not have sprung up, wants which grow and strengthen, and overpower, until reason and common sense are swept away as with a flood, and the reign of unrestraint sets in, to the end of a complete brutalization, and to prevent such results or any approach to them, the expedient of the book is proposed, as offering a comparatively easy remedy ; for a quaint writer says : ' When a man has once got in the rapids of Niagara, the next thing he will do, will be to go over the falls. Having once got in, there is no possibilty of getting out. The way for him to escape going over, is not to get in the rapids. When a man has once put a spark to powder, he need not clap his hand upon it to prevent it from going off. It will do no good. The only way for him to keep it from going off, is to keep the spark away from it. Many men can let the cup alone if they keep away from it, who cannot if they go where it is. Many men can abstain from lust, if they do not go within the circuit of its malaria, who cannot free themselves from it, after they have once been infected by it. Many men can control their temper, so long as they avoid everything calculated to arouse it, who have no power over it, after it has once become aroused. Many of our dispositions must be taken care of beforehand, not afterwards. And when they have led us into wrong courses, our error consists, not in the fact, that we could not keep ourselves, but in the fact that we did not learn enough about ourselves to know that some parts of our nature were not to be exposed; that some parts of our nature must be carried with watching, with vigilant fore-looking.' The great principle is well put here, that to avoid excesses, we must not put ourselves in the way of a too easy indulgence of what is allowable. If all the evils which arise from any kind of over-indulgence, ended in the persons who practice them, it would be comparatively speaking, a happy thing; but they are far-reaching in their pernicious influences; they extend beyond those who practice, and are carried into the ages to come, destined to be a blight on generations yet unborn.

"All excesses beget debility of the organs connected with them, and these organs, whether they be the lungs, the stomach, the liver, or any others, will always, under this excessive action or stimulation, prepare a vitiated, imperfect material, diseased and monstrous, according to circumstances. Hence the multitude of weakly, sickly, puny persons in every direction; muscles flabby, bones slight, face wan, gait unstable, and the whole 'physique' an abortion. As to the moral nature there is a blight over it all—a wanting to be something, without an ability to be anything—fickle, wayward, and unfixed; while in another direction there are low inclinations, vicious tendencies, degrading practices, and a general lack of all that is high and noble and elevating. As to the mind of those begotten in brutalizing indulgences, it is without strength, without persistence of purpose, and without either the capacity or the desire for high culture and exalted aims Thus the whole nature, physical, mental and moral, is a blight, a blot, a blank. That the characteristics of the future being, in body and brain and heart, are colored by those of the parents, which prevail about the time of reproduction, is conceded by scientific men, and demonstrated by facts. A Massachusetts state paper, on 'Lunacy,' reports that four-fifths of the idiotic children, were those of parents, one or both of whom lived in habits of drunkenness—indicating that children begotten in the stupor of debauch, will have a vacuity of mind for life. On the other hand, it is known that the mother of the first Napoleon, for months before he was born, accompanied her soldier husband in his martial expeditions, and traversed the country side by side with him on horseback, thus sharing in all his toils. Hannah of old, conceived and carried Samuel, while her whole nature was imbued with a deep religious devotion, under the influence of which she consecrated the future prophet to the supreme service of his Maker. It would seem then to be a wise forethought, that perpetuation should be accomplished under favoring conditions of mind and body ; the latter in high health, invigorated by a regular, unbroken and refreshing sleep, the blood all pure, by an eight or ten hours breathing of fresh, life-giving air ; while the former, fully aroused to a sense of high responsibilities, the heart and the affections, at the same time, loving and pure, would present a combination of desirable circumstances, which could not possibly be hoped for in any other way than by the expedient which the idea of the book proposes, whereby everything could be made a subject of deliberate, thoughtful, and rational calculation, and surprise, in moments of mental, moral and physical unfitness, would be impossible."

APPENDIX H.

WE continue this extract from Margaret Fuller's "Women of the Nineteenth Century," in order to show the elevating effects of a high moral and intellectual culture on woman. While the father ignores his duties and his responsibilities, and the rights of his daughter to the highest development of her best capacities, he must expect evidences of weakness and folly as the legitimate fruits of such abnegation.*

"Whenever religion (I mean the thirst for truth and good, not the love of sect and dogma,) had its course, the original design was apprehended in its simplicity, and the dove presaged sweetly from Didona's oak. I was talking on this subject with Miranda, a woman who, if any in the world, could speak without heat and bitterness of the position of her sex. Her father was a man who cherished no sentimental reverence for woman, but a full belief in the equality of the sex. She was his oldest child, and came to him when he needed a companion. From the time she could speak and go alone he addressed her not as a plaything but as a living mind. Among the few verses he ever wrote was a copy addressed to this child when the first

---

* The rights of children are clearly defined by Herbert Spencer in his recent work on "Education," to which excellent and useful book we refer the reader.

locks were cut from her head, and the reverence he expressed on this occasion for that cherished head he never belied. It was to him the temple of an immortal intellect. He respected his child, however, too much to be an indulgent parent. He called on her for clear judgment, for courage, for honor and fidelity; in short, for such virtues as he knew. In so far as he possessed the keys to the wonders of the universe, he allowed free use of them to her, and by the incentive of a high expectation, he forbade, as far as possible, that she should let the privilege lie idle.

" Thus the child was early led to feel herself a child of the spirit. She took her place easily, not only in the world of organized being, but in the world of mind. A dignified sense of self-dependence was given as all her portion, and she found it a sure anchor. Herself securely anchored, her relations with others were established with equal security. She was fortunate in a total absence of those charms which would have drawn to her bewildering flatteries, and in a strong electric nature which repelled those who did not belong to her, and attracted those who did. With men and women her relations were noble—affectionate without passion, intellectual without coldness. The world was free to her, and she lived freely in it. Outward adversity came, and inward conflict, but that faith and self-respect had been early awakened which always leads at last to an outward serenity and an inward peace.

" Of Miranda I had always thought as an example that the restraints upon the sex were insuperable only to those who think them so, or to those who noisily strive to break them. She had taken a course of her own, and no man stood in her way. Many of her acts had been unusual, but they excited no uproar. Few helped, but none checked her, and the many men who knew her mind and her life, showed to her confidence as to a brother, gentleness as to a sister. And not only refined but very coarse men approved and aided one in whom they saw resolution and clearness of design. Her mind was often the leading one, always effective.

"When I talked with her upon these matters, and had said very much what I have written, she smiling replied,

And yet we must admit that I have been fortunate, and this should not be. My good father's early trust gave the first bias, and the rest followed, of course. It is true that I have had less outward aid in after years than most women, but that is of little consequence. Religion was early awakened in my soul, and a sense that what the soul is capable to ask it must attain, and that, though I might be aided and instructed by others, I must depend on myself as the only constant friend. This self-dependence, which was honored in me, is deprecated as a fault in most women. They are taught to learn their rule from without, not to unfold it from within.

"'This is the fault of man, who is still vain, and wishes to be more important to woman, than by right he ought to be.'

"'Men have not shown this disposition towards you,' I said.

"'No! because the position I early was enabled to take, was one of self-denial. And were all women as sure of their wants as I was, the result would be the same. But they are so overloaded with precepts by guardians, who think that nothing is so much to be dreaded for a woman as originality of thought or character, that their minds are impeded by doubts till they lose their chance of fair free proportions. The difficulty is to get them to the point from which they shall naturally develope self respect, and learn self help.

"'Once I thought that men would help to forward this

state of things more than I do now. I saw so many of them wretched in the connexions they had formed in weakness and vanity. They seemed so glad to esteem women whenever they could.

" ' The soft arms of affection, said one of the most discerning spirits, will not suffice for me, unless on them I see the steel bracelets of strength.

" ' But early I perceived that men never, in any extreme of despair, wished to be women. On the contrary, they were ever ready to taunt one another at any sign of weakness, with—Art thou not like the woman who——

" ' The passage ends various ways, according to the occasion, and the rhetoric of the speaker. When they admired any woman they were inclined to speak of her as " above her sex." Silently I observed this, and feared it argued a rooted scepticism, which for ages had been fastening on the heart, and which only an age of miracles could eradicate. Ever I have been treated with great sincerity; and I look upon it as a signal instance of this, that an intimate friend of the other sex said, in a fervent moment, that I " deserved in some star to be a man." He was much surprised when I disclosed my view of my position and hopes, when I declared my faith of the feminine side; the side of love, of beauty, of holiness, was now to have its full chance, and that, if either were better, it was better now to be a woman, for even the slightest achievement of good was furthering an especial work of our time. He smiled incredulous. " She makes the best she can of it," thought he. " Let Jews believe the pride of Jewry, but I am of the better sort, and know better."

" ' Another used as high praise, in speaking of a character in literature, the words " a manly woman." So in the noble passage of Ben Jonson :

"'I meant the day-star should not brighter rise,
   Nor shed like influence from its lucent seat;
I meant she should be courteous, facile, sweet,
   Free from that solemn vice of greatness, pride;
I meant each softest virtue there should meet,
   Fit in that softer bosom to abide;
Only a learned and a *manly soul*
   I purposed her, that should with even powers
The rock, the spindle, and the shears control
   Of destiny, and spin her own free hours.'"

APPENDIX I.

EDUCATION FOR PARENTHOOD.

From "Physical Education," by Herbert Spencer.

"IF by some strange chance not a vestige of us descended to the remote future save a pile of our school books, or some college examination papers, we may imagine how puzzled an antiquary of the period would be, on finding in them no indication that the learners were ever likely to be parents. 'This must be the *curriculum* for their celibates,' we may fancy him concluding. 'I perceive here an elaborate preparation for many things: especially for reading the books of extinct nations and of co-existing nations, (from which indeed it seems clear that these people had very little worth reading in their own tongue,) but I find no reference whatever to the bringing up of children. They could not have been so absurd as to omit all training for this gravest of responsibilities. Evidently then, this was the school course of one of their monastic orders.'

" Seriously is it not an astonishing fact, that though on the treatment of offspring depend their lives or deaths, and their moral welfare or ruin, yet not one word of instruction on the treatment of offspring is ever given to those who will hereafter be parents? Is it not monstrous that the fate of a new generation should be left to the chances of unreasoning custom, impulse, fancy—joined with the suggestions of ignorant nurses, and the prejudiced counsel of grandmothers? If a merchant commenced business without any knowledge of arithmetic and book-keeping, we should exclaim at his folly, and look for disastrous consequences. Or if, before studying anatomy, a man set up as surgical operator, we should wonder at his audacity, and pity his patients. But that parents should begin the difficult task of rearing children without ever having given a thought to the principles—physical, moral and intellectual—which ought to guide them, excites neither surprise at the actors, nor pity for their victims.

"To tens of thousands that are killed, add hundreds of thousands that survive with feeble constitutions, and millions that grow up with constitutions not so strong as they should be—and you will have some idea of the curse inflicted on their offspring by parents ignorant of the laws of life. Do but consider for a moment that the regimen to which children are subject is hourly telling upon them to their life-long injury or benefit, and that there are twenty ways of going wrong to one way of going right, and you will get some idea of the enormous mischief that is almost every where inflicted by the thoughtless, hap-hazard system in common use. Is it decided that a boy shall be clothed in some flimsy short dress, and be allowed to go playing about with limbs reddened with cold? The decision will tell on his whole future existence—either in illness or in stunted growth, or in deficient energy, or in a maturity less vigorous than it ought to have been, and consequent hindrances to success and happiness. Are children doomed to a monotonous dietary, or a dietary deficient in nutritiveness? Their ultimate physical power, and their efficiency as men and women, will inevitably be more or less diminished by it.

Are they forbidden vociferous play, or (being too ill-clothed to bear exposure) are they kept in-doors in cold weather? They are certain to fall below that measure of health and strength to which they would have attained. When sons and daughters grow up sickly and feeble, parents commonly regard the event as a misfortune—as a visitation of Providence. Thinking after the prevalent chaotic fashion, they assume that these evils come without causes, or that the causes are supernatural. Nothing of the kind. In some cases the causes are doubtless inherited, but in most cases foolish regulations are the causes. Very generally parents themselves are responsible for all this pain, this debility, this depression, this misery. They have undertaken to control the lives of their offspring from hour to hour, with cruel carelessness they have neglected to learn anything about these vital processes which they are unceasingly affecting by their commands and prohibitions; in utter ignorance of the simplest physiologic laws, they have been year by year undermining the constitutions of their children, and have so inflicted disease and premature death not only on them but on their descendants.

" Equally great are the ignorance and the consequent injury, when we turn from physical training to moral training. Consider the young mother and her nursery legislation. But a few years ago she was at school, where her memory was crammed with words, and names, and dates, and her reflective faculties scarcely in the slightest degree exercised—where not one idea was given her respecting the methods of dealing with the opening mind of childhood; and where her discipline did not in the least fit her for thinking out methods of her own. The intervening years have been spent in practising music, in fancy work, in novel reading, and in party-going; no thought having yet been given to the grave responsibilities of maternity; and scarcely any of that solid intellectual culture obtained which would be some preparation for such responsibilities. And now see her with an unfolding human character committed to her charge—see her profoundly ignorant of the phenomena with which she has to deal, undertaking to do that which can be done but imperfectly, even with the aid of the profoundest knowledge. She knows nothing about the nature of the emotions, their order of evolution, their functions, or where use ends and abuse begins. She is under the impression that some of the feelings are wholly bad, which is not true of any one of them; and that others are good, however far they may be carried, which is also not true of any one of them. And then, ignorant as she is of that with which she has to deal, she is equally ignorant of the effects that will be produced on it by this or that treatment. What can be more inevitable than the disastrous results we see hourly arising? Lacking knowledge of mental phenomena, with their causes and consequences, her interference is frequently more mischievous than absolute passivity would have been. This and that action, which are quite normal and benificial, she frequently thwarts, and so diminishes the child's happiness and profit, injures its temper and her own, and produces estrangement. Deeds which she thinks it desirable to encourage, she gets performed by threats and bribes, or by exciting a desire for applause; considering little what the inward motive may be, so long as the outward conduct conforms; and thus cultivating hypocrisy, and fear and selfishness in place of good feeling. While insisting on truthfulness, she constantly sets an example of untruth by threatening penalties which she does not inflict. While inculcating self-control, she hourly visits on her little ones angry scoldings for acts that do not call for them. She has not the remotest idea that in the nursery as in the world, that alone is the truly salutary discipline which on all conduct, good and bad, the natural consequences—the consequences, pleasurable or painful, which in the nature of things such conduct tends to bring. Being thus without theoretic guidance, and quite incapable of guiding herself by tracing the mental processes going on in her children, her rule is impulsive, inconsistent, mischievous, often in the highest degree, and would indeed be generally ruinous, were it not that the overwhelming tendency of the growing mind to assume the moral type of the race usually subordinates all minor influences.

"And then the culture of the intellect—is not this, too, mismanaged in a similar manner? Grant that the phenomena of intelligence conforms to laws; grant that the evolution of intelligence in a child also conforms to laws; and it follows inevitably that education can be rightly guided only by a knowledge of those laws. To suppose that you can properly regulate this process of forming and accumulating ideas, without understanding the nature of the process is absurd. How widely then, must teaching as it is, differ from teaching as it should be; when hardly any parents, and but very few teachers, know anything about psychology. As might be expected, the system is grievously at fault, alike in matter and in manner. While the right class of facts are withheld, the wrong class is forcibly administered in the wrong way and in the wrong order. With that common limited idea of education which confines it to knowledge gained from books, parents thrust primers into the hands of their little ones years to soon, to their great injury. Not recognising the truth that the function of books is suplementary—that they form an indirect means to knowledge when direct means fail —a means of seeing through other men what you cannot see for yourself; they are eager to give second hand facts in place of the first hand facts. Not perceiving the enormous value of that spontaneous education which goes on in early years—not perceiving that a child's restless observation, instead of being ignored or checked, should be diligently administered to, and made as accurate and complete as possible, they insist in occupying the eyes and thoughts with things that are, for the time being, incomprehensible and repugnant. Possessed by a superstition that worships the symbols of knowledge instead of the knowledge itself, they do not see that only when his acquaintance with the objects and processes of the household, the streets, and the fields, is becoming tolerably exhaustive—only then should a child be introduced to the new sources of information which books supply : and this, not only because immediate cognition is of far greater value than mediate cognition ; but also, because the words contained in books can be rightly interpreted into ideas, only in proportion to the antecedent experience of things. Observe next, that this formal instruction, far too soon commenced, is carried on with little reference to the laws of development. Intellectual progress is of necessity from the concrete to the abstract. But regardless of this, highly abstract subjects, such as grammar, which should come quite late, are begun quite early. Political geography, dead and uninteresting to a child, and which should be an appendage to sociological studies is commenced betimes ; while physical geography, comprehensible and comparatively attractive to a child, is in great part passed over. Nearly every subject is arranged in abnormal order : definitions, and rules, and principles being put first, instead of being disclosed, as they are in the order of nature, through the study of cases. And then, pervading the whole is the vicious system of rote learning—a system of sacrificing the spirit to the letter. See the results. What with perceptions unnaturally dulled by early thwarting, and coerced attention to books—what with the mental confusion produced by teaching subjects before they can be understood, and in each of them giving generalizations before the facts of which these are the generalizations—what with making the pupil a mere passive recipient of other's ideas, and not in the least leading him to be an active inquirer or self-instructor—and what with taxing the faculties to excess, there are very few minds that become as efficient as they might be. Examinations being once passed, books are laid aside; the greater part of what has been acquired, being unorganized, soon drops out of recollection; what remains is mostly inert—the art of applying knowledge not having been cultivated; and there is but little power either of accurate observation or independent thinking. To which add, that while much of the information is of relatively small value, an immense amount of information of transcendent value is entirely passed over."

APPENDIX J.

In treating of the evils which curse society, and impede human development, we must not overlook tobacco—the pernicious source and origin of many ills. If rum has slain its thousands, tobacco has enslaved its tens of thousands; making them grovel before it in the most abject and demoralizing vassalage. The king and the peasant, the president and the plow boy, have been alike its victims; and I hazard nothing in saying that while it has poisoned their bodies, it has depraved their souls. The discovery of America has, doubtless, been a great blessing to mankind; yet the truth that there is no earthly good unmixed with evil, might be summed up tersely, in the simple phrase—America gave to civilization her tobacco. Effete China may have smoked herself stupid before Columbus searched for his new passage to the Indies—but Europe, at least, was ignorant of the existence of this vile weed; which proves to be a stimulant to all vices, and a narcotic to all virtues.

It is not necessary to write an elaborate essay upon the nature and effects of this poisonous production; that has been done by abler pens—some of them writing from the depths of a bitter experience. The use of tobacco has been satirized by the keenest wits; but the inherent vulgarity which attaches to every mode in which it is taken, can never be strongly enough expressed by any language. When the caricaturist would represent a coarse, unmannerly woman, he pictures her smoking a cigar; I do not know that the boldest, has ever dared so to malign her, as to represent her chewing a quid. This fact is more than ample to illustrate the aesthetics of tobacco. Doubtless, there are great and good men who are addicted to its use; but they were not great, nor greatly good, when they commenced the practice. Many gentlemen take a cigar after dinner, in order, they say, to promote digestion; but if they did not indulge their appetites to repletion, the antidote would not be required.

Of all the modes of using tobacco, that of chewing is decidedly the vilest—the most unnatural—and at its first introduction to a human palate the most artificially forced, to create a taste for its instrinsically repugnant and noxious qualities. He who has achieved a victory over Nature, by this desecration of one of his five senses, not only pollutes his mouth, but the very air he breathes, and thus makes himself personally offensive to others. This use of tobacco is, in its entailed effects, and consequences, highly detrimental to the nervous system, and to the whole constitution, as it promotes an unnatural discharge of saliva, and other secretions, so essential to a perfect digestion. Hence the pale and cadaverous faces—the lean and dyspeptic aspect, of its self-immolated victims. Again, the constant and unnatural expectoration attending this habit, engenders an habitual thirst and craving for alcoholic stimulants, leading to drunkenness and all its bitter concomitants.

"It is enough to say, that there are very few gross, bad men, who do not use tobacco. Go into the lowest purlieus of vice and poverty, in the midst of theft, beggary, and starvation—in the midst of nameless degradation, and indescribable filth, there tobacco always abounds.

The use of tobacco is one of the very worst forms of stimulating the human system—*the* most filthy; and has a steadily debasing tendency in its moral effects. While it does not produce intoxication, it stultifies all the finer sensibilities, by unduly exciting every grosser appetite and craving, which belongs merely to the physical being

Unfortunately we have no "line or plummet," wherewith to measure the vitiating effects arising from the use of this pernicious plant; if we had, we should discover that every ounce of tobacco taken into the circulation would show a depreciation in the mental and moral tone of its victim. Like all inherited tendencies, this debasing influence descends as do other " sins of the fathers, even to the third and fourth generations." Now the same beneficent laws of inheritance, which insure symmetry and fair proportions when allowed their legitimate action—will when thus perverted by vice and ignorance, degrade and stultify the innocent offspring. In the abodes of vice and poverty may be seen pitiable little weaklings, defrauded of their birthright—health and strength—deprived of all that makes life joyous—martyrs to an ignoble propensity of degraded parents.

The subject treated in these pages is so vast and many-sided that new points are constantly presenting themselves, both from speculative thought upon it, and from the actual experience of every day.

Another of the many evils which stand in the way of a harmonious development of offspring, arises from an arbitrary, controling spirit, and a too penurious habit of some husbands and fathers. It would seem that men in our day, if never before, must see the pernicious effects upon their children and society, of many of the kinds of tyranny habitually exercised over women.

Woman's and humanity's great need in maternity, is the

loving harmonious state of mind. Now it is not in the soul that is only human, to love or respect the agents of opression and injustice—those by which it suffers humiliation and defeat, not only of its reasonable, but of its noblest purposes. In pecuniary matters alone, women in American society are too often treated in a spirit quite the opposite to that which could inspire an increasing love, and noble trust in the fathers of their children. There is many a patient, enduring mother in our midst, doing her imperishable lifework—giving birth to and rearing her children, who has not the freedom in money matters, that her son has, although in his teens; because he is a man and she only a woman. It is assumed in behalf of his coming manhood, that he has need of a certain freedom in this regard, if he is to grow manly; while her need may be quite ignored so far as she cannot enforce it by entreaties, cajolery, or sulking and downright grieving. Women do not always spend money wisely, or worthily; neither do men. Yet is it not of less importance that some women should abuse their trust in such matters, than that one sensitive confiding wife should suffer injustice, and have the souls of her children cramped and dwarfed through her starved intellect, and her thwarted aspirations to attain for them something greater than she, unaided, has the ability or power to bestow?

The most effectual way to educate women to a rational, a noble use of money, is to allow them the uncontroled posession of a reasonable amount of it. Such trust and confidence would, in most cases, insure a sense of responsibility for its wise employment. Women have demonstrated their executive, and financial abilities too often to have them doubted in this age of the world. Miss Martineau, in her journal of observation through the Southern States, affirms that the plantations owned by women were the most orderly, the most productive, and the best managed of any that came under her observation.

The prudent conduct of widows, in bringing up their families, and in improving their estates is proverbial. A New England mother or sister will work her fingers to the bone, in order to give a bright ambitious son or brother a liberal education, and to place him in a position, whereby he may do credit to himself, and reflect honor on his family.

Moreover, if it were the practice of men engaged in business to settle some portion of property on their wives, (during their prosperity,) the commercial panics, with which our country is so frequently convulsed, would not, as heretofore, leave them destitute, and entail a degenerate condition on their children, thus retarding civilization and progressive development.

NEW BOOKS
And New Editions Recently Issued by
CARLETON, PUBLISHER,
(Late RUDD & CARLETON,)
413 *BROADWAY, NEW YORK.*

N.B.—THE PUBLISHER, upon receipt of the price in advance, will send any of the following Books, by mail, POSTAGE FREE, to any part of the United States. This convenient and very safe mode may be adopted when the neighboring Booksellers are not supplied with the desired work. State name and address in full.

Les Miserables.
Victor Hugo's great novel—the only complete unabridged translation. Library Edition. Five vols. 12mo. cloth, each, $1.00.
The same, five vols. 8vo. cloth, $1.00. Paper covers, 50 cts.
The same, (cheap ed.) 1 vol. 8vo. cloth, $1.50. paper, $1.00.
Les Miserables—Illustrations.
26 photographic illustrations, by Brion. Elegant quarto, $3.00
Among the Pines,
or, Down South in Secession Time. Cloth, $1.00, paper, 75 cts.
My Southern Friends.
By author of "Among the Pines." Cloth, $1.00. paper, 75 cts.
Rutledge.
A powerful American novel, by an unknown author, $1.50.
The Sutherlands.
The new novel by the popular author of "Rutledge," $1.50.
The Habits of Good Society.
A hand-book for ladies and gentlemen. Best, wittiest, most entertaining work on taste and good manners ever printed, $1.50
The Cloister and the Hearth.
A magnificent new historical novel, by Charles Reade, author of "Peg Woffington," etc., cloth, $1.50, paper covers, $1.25
Beulah.
A novel of remarkable power, by Miss A. J. Evans. $1.50

Artemus Ward, His Book.
The racy writings of this humorous author. Illustrated, $1.25.

The Old Merchants of New York.
Entertaining reminiscences of ancient mercantile New York City, by "Walter Barrett, clerk." First Series. $1.50 each.

Like and Unlike.
Novel by A. S. Roe, author of "I've been thinking," &c. $1 50.

Orpheus C. Kerr Papers.
Second series of letters by this comic military authority. $1.25

Marian Grey.
New domestic novel, by the author of "Lena Rivers," etc. $1.50.

Lena Rivers.
A popular American novel, by Mrs. Mary J. Holmes, $1.50.

A Book about Doctors.
An entertaining volume about the medical profession. $1.50.

The Adventures of Verdant Green.
Humorous novel of English College life. Illustrated. $1.25.

The Culprit Fay.
Joseph Rodman Drake's faery poem, elegantly printed, 50 cts.

Doctor Antonio.
A charming love-tale of Italian life, by G. Ruffini, $1.50.

Lavinia.
A new love-story, by the author of "Doctor Antonio," $1.50.

Deer Experience.
An amusing Parisian novel, by author "Doctor Antonio," $1.00.

The Life of Alexander Von Humboldt.
A new and popular biography of this *savant*, including his travels and labors, with introduction by Bayard Taylor, $1.50.

Love (L'Amour.)
A remarkable volume, from the French of Michelet. $1.25.

Woman (La Femme.)
A continuation of "Love (L'Amour)," by same author, $1.25

The Sea (La Mer.)
New work by Michelet, author "Love" and "Woman," $1.25

The Moral History of Woman.
Companion to Michelet's "L'Amour," from the French, $1.25

Mother Goose for Grown Folks.
Humorous and satirical rhymes for grown people, 75 cts.

The Kelly's and the O'Kelly's.
Novel by Anthony Trollope, author of "Doctor Thorne," $1.50

The Great Tribulation.
Or, Things coming on the earth, by Rev. John Cumming, D.D., author "Apocalyptic Sketches," etc., two series, each $1.00.

The Great Preparation.
Or, Redemption draweth nigh, by Rev. John Cumming, D.D., author "The Great Tribulation," etc., two series, each $1.00.

The Great Consummation.
Sequel "Great Tribulation," Dr. Cumming, two series, $1.00.

Teach us to Pray.
A new work on The Lord's Prayer, by Dr. Cumming, $1.00.

The Slave Power.
By Jas. E. Cairnes, of Dublin University, Lond. ed. $1.25.

Game Fish of the North.
A sporting work for Northern States and Canada. Illus., $1.50.

Drifting About.
By Stephen C. Massett ("Jeemes Pipes"), illustrated, $1.25

The Flying Dutchman.
A humorous Poem by John G. Saxe, with illustrations, 50 cts.

Notes on Shakspeare.
By Jas. H. Hackett, the American Comedian (portrait), $1.50.

The Spirit of Hebrew Poetry.
By Isaac Taylor, author "History of Enthusiasm," etc., $2.00.

A Life of Hugh Miller.
Author of "Testimony of the Rocks," &c., new edition, $1.50.

A Woman's Thoughts about Women.
By Miss Dinah Mulock, author of "John Halifax," etc., $1.00.

Curiosities of Natural History.
An entertaining vol., by F. T. Buckland; two series, each $1.25

The Partisan Leader.
Beverley Tucker's notorious Southern Disunion novel, $1.25

Cesar Birotteau.
First of a series of Honore de Balzac's best French novels, $1.00.

Petty Annoyances of Married Life.
The second of the series of Balzac's best French novels, $1.00.

The Alchemist.
The third of the series of the best of Balzac's novels, $1.00

Eugenie Grandet.
The fourth of the series of Balzac's best French novels, $1.00

The National School for the Soldier.
Elementary work for the soldier; by Capt. Van Ness, 50 cts.

Tom Tiddler's Ground.
Charles Dickens's new Christmas Story, paper cover, 25 cts.
National Hymns.
An essay by Richard Grant White. 8vo. embellished, $1.00.
George Brimley.
Literary Essays reprinted from the British Quarterlies, $1.25
Thomas Bailey Aldrich.
First complete collection of Poems, blue and gold binding, $1.00.
Out of His Head.
A strange and eccentric romance by T. B. Aldrich, $1.00.
The Course of True Love
Never did run smooth. A Poem by Thomas B. Aldrich, 50 cts.
Poems of a Year.
By Thomas B. Aldrich, author of "Babie Bell," &c., 75 cts.
The King's Bell.
A Mediæval Legend in verse, by R. H. Stoddard, 75 cts.
The Morgesons.
A clever novel of American Life, by Mrs. R. H. Stoddard, $1.00.
Beatrice Cenci.
An historical novel by F. D. Guerrazzi, from the Italian, $1.50.
Isabella Orsini.
An historical novel by the author of "Beatrice Cenci," $1.25.
A Popular Treatise on Deafness.
For individuals and families, by E. B. Lighthill, M.D., $1.00.
Oriental Harems and Scenery.
A gossipy work, translated from the French of Belgiojoso, $1.25.
Lola Montez.
Her lectures and autobiography, with a steel portrait, $1.25.
John Doe and Richard Roe.
A novel of New York city life, by Edward S. Gould, $1.00.
Doesticks' Letters.
The original letters of this great humorist, illustrated, $1.50.
Plu-ri-bus-tah.
A comic history of America, by "Doesticks," illus., $1.50.
The Elephant Club.
A humorous description of club-life, by "Doesticks," $1.50.
Vernon Grove.
A novel by Mrs. Caroline H. Glover, Charleston, S. C., $1.00
The Book of Chess Literature.
A complete Encyclopædia of this subject, by D. W. Fiske, $1.50.

www.ingramcontent.com/pod-product-compliance
Lightning Source LLC
Chambersburg PA
CBHW032148230426
43672CB00011B/2488